Java: From Beginner to Expert

A Complete Guide to Mastering Java Programming Language

BOOZMAN RICHARD

BOOKER BLUNT

Table of Content

TABLE OF CONTENTS

INTRODUCTION

Java: From Beginner to Expert – A Comprehensive Guide to Mastering Java Programming

Java is one of the most widely used programming languages in the world, known for its versatility, security, and powerful capabilities across multiple platforms. Whether you're interested in building desktop applications, mobile apps, web applications, or even complex enterprise solutions, Java provides a robust foundation for developers to create scalable, secure, and high-performance applications.

This book, *Java: From Beginner to Expert*, is designed to be the ultimate guide for anyone looking to master Java, from those just starting their journey to those who want to refine and extend their existing skills. This comprehensive guide takes you step-by-step through the essential concepts, tools, and frameworks that every Java developer needs to know. Each chapter builds on the previous one, ensuring you gain a deep understanding of Java's core concepts while giving you the hands-on experience necessary to become an expert.

Why This Book?

1. **Beginner-Friendly**: This book starts with the basics of Java and programming concepts. It covers foundational concepts like variables, data types, control flow, object-oriented programming (OOP), and working with data. Even if you've never written a line of code before, you'll find a structured, approachable path to learning Java.

2. **Hands-On Projects**: Learning by doing is the most effective approach, which is why this book includes practical, real-world examples in every chapter. From building simple programs to creating fully functional Java applications, you'll gain practical coding experience that can be applied to your own projects.

3. **Comprehensive Coverage**: This book covers everything from the core Java language to advanced topics such as **multithreading**, **network programming**, **JavaFX** for GUI applications, and **Spring Boot** for building modern, scalable web applications. Whether you want to work with databases, APIs, or design user interfaces, this book will guide you through it.

8

4. **Best Practices**: You'll learn not only how to write Java code but also **how to write clean, efficient, and secure code**. Best practices for handling exceptions, ensuring performance optimization, and protecting your applications from security threats are covered in detail.

5. **Real-World Examples**: Each chapter of this book presents real-world use cases and practical examples, including building a simple inventory management system, a task manager application with JavaFX, and a full-fledged e-commerce website using Spring Boot. By the end of the book, you'll have created several applications and projects that demonstrate your mastery of Java.

6. **From Desktop to Web and Beyond**: Java's reach is vast, and this book embraces its versatility. You'll start by building simple desktop applications with JavaFX, then progress to web development with **Spring Boot**, work with databases using **JDBC**, and implement powerful security measures to safeguard your applications. You'll also gain an understanding of **RESTful APIs** and how to connect your Java applications to external systems.

What You Will Learn

Part 1: Core Java Concepts
We begin with an in-depth look at the fundamental building blocks of Java. You'll learn about:

- Basic syntax and structure
- Data types, variables, and control flow mechanisms (loops, conditionals)
- Object-Oriented Programming (OOP) principles: inheritance, polymorphism, encapsulation, and abstraction
- Exception handling and debugging techniques

Part 2: Advanced Java Topics
After mastering the fundamentals, we move into more complex subjects like:

- **Multithreading and concurrency**: How to write multi-threaded applications for better performance
- **Working with files and data**: Reading and writing files, handling input/output, and processing data
- **Collections and data structures**: Working with arrays, lists, sets, maps, and more
- **Generics**: Writing flexible and type-safe code

Part 3: Java for Web Development

Java is not only used for desktop applications but also for powerful web applications. This part dives deep into:

- Building web applications using **Servlets** and **JSP** (JavaServer Pages)
- Developing RESTful web services with **Spring Boot** for creating microservices
- **Spring Security** for managing authentication and authorization

Part 4: Data Handling and Database Integration

You'll learn how to store, retrieve, and manipulate data using:

- **JDBC** (Java Database Connectivity) for interacting with relational databases
- **Hibernate and ORM (Object-Relational Mapping)** for working with data more effectively
- **Spring Data JPA** for simplified data access and management

Part 5: Java Security and Best Practices

Security is an essential aspect of any application. In this section, you'll explore:

11

- **Password hashing and encryption** to secure sensitive user data
- **Best practices for secure, efficient Java code**: Input validation, minimizing vulnerabilities, and using encryption techniques
- Handling **common security threats** like SQL injection, cross-site scripting (XSS), and session hijacking

Part 6: JavaFX and Desktop Application Development

Learn how to create beautiful and interactive desktop applications using **JavaFX**, including:

- Building user interfaces with buttons, text fields, and complex layouts
- Implementing event handling to make applications interactive
- Creating desktop apps that manage user data, like a task manager or inventory management system

Part 7: Putting It All Together – Capstone Project

In the final project, you'll integrate everything you've learned into a real-world application. This includes:

- Designing and coding a fully functional e-commerce website or mobile app
- Implementing all the core concepts, such as web development, database integration, security, and UI design

Why This Book Is Different

1. **Real-World Application**: This book is not just about theoretical concepts. You will build actual applications that solve real-world problems, making it easier to understand how Java is used in the industry.

2. **Step-by-Step Guidance**: Each concept is broken down and explained in detail, with plenty of examples and code snippets. Even if you're a beginner, you will understand the practical application of each concept.

3. **Practical Projects**: By working on hands-on projects like building a task manager, inventory management system, and e-commerce app, you'll gain the confidence to work on any Java project.

Who Is This Book For?

This book is ideal for:

- **Beginners**: If you're new to Java, this book will guide you step-by-step from the basics to advanced topics. You will start with simple programs and gradually work your way up to complex applications.
- **Intermediate Developers**: If you already have some Java knowledge, this book will expand your understanding by introducing advanced concepts, best practices, and modern Java frameworks.
- **Aspiring Software Engineers**: If you're looking to start a career in Java development, this book will equip you with the practical skills and knowledge needed to build professional-grade applications.

Conclusion

Java: From Beginner to Expert is the ultimate guide to becoming proficient in Java programming. By the end of this book, you'll have the knowledge and confidence to build and deploy Java applications of any complexity. Whether you're developing desktop applications, working on the backend of a web service, or building enterprise-level solutions, this book will provide you with the tools you need to succeed in the world of Java development.

Let's embark on this journey of mastering Java, and build amazing applications together!

Part 1

Introduction to Java

Programming

CHAPTER 1

GETTING STARTED WITH JAVA

Introduction to Java: Why Java is Still One of the Most Popular Programming Languages

Java has remained one of the most popular programming languages for over two decades, largely due to its reliability, scalability, and portability. Originally developed by Sun Microsystems in 1995, Java was designed to be platform-independent, meaning programs written in Java can run on any device that has a Java Virtual Machine (JVM) installed. This "write once, run anywhere" philosophy became a game-changer for developers, making Java the go-to choice for building cross-platform applications.

Over the years, Java has evolved into a versatile language that supports a wide range of applications, from mobile apps to enterprise systems and cloud-based services. Some reasons why Java continues to be in high demand include:

- **Cross-Platform Compatibility:** Java's portability allows it to run on any operating system with the JVM.

- **Robust Ecosystem:** With an extensive array of libraries, frameworks, and tools, Java offers everything developers need to create applications efficiently.
- **Community Support:** Java has one of the largest, most active developer communities, offering support, tutorials, and open-source projects.
- **Performance:** While Java is not as fast as languages like C++, its Just-In-Time (JIT) compiler, garbage collection, and performance optimizations ensure that it meets the demands of modern applications.

Java's widespread use in various domains, including enterprise systems (e.g., banking and financial systems), web applications, Android development, and large-scale data processing, underscores its relevance in the software development world.

Setting Up the Java Development Environment: Installing JDK, Configuring Your IDE, and Writing Your First Java Program

Before diving into coding, you need to set up the tools that will help you write and execute Java programs. Here's how you can get started:

1. **Install Java Development Kit (JDK)**

- o The JDK is a software package that includes everything you need to compile, run, and debug Java applications. It contains the Java Runtime Environment (JRE), compilers, and various development tools.
- o **Step 1:** Go to the Oracle JDK download page and download the appropriate version of the JDK for your operating system.
- o **Step 2:** Follow the installation instructions based on your platform (Windows, macOS, or Linux).
- o **Step 3:** After installation, check if Java is correctly installed by running `java -version` in your terminal or command prompt. If installed correctly, it should display the Java version number.

2. **Choose and Install an Integrated Development Environment (IDE)**
   - o While you can write Java code in any text editor, using an IDE makes the process much easier by offering features like code completion, syntax highlighting, debugging, and more.
   - o Popular Java IDEs include:
     - **IntelliJ IDEA** (Free and paid versions)
     - **Eclipse** (Open-source and free)
     - **NetBeans** (Free, open-source IDE)

19

- o Download and install the IDE of your choice from their official websites. Once installed, configure the IDE to point to the JDK you installed.

3. **Writing Your First Java Program: "Hello, World!"**

   - o Open your IDE and create a new Java project. Inside the project, create a new Java file and name it `HelloWorld.java` (file names in Java should always match the class name).

   - o Type the following code inside your new Java file:

```java
public class HelloWorld {
    public static void main(String[] args) {
        System.out.println("Hello,
World!");
    }
}
```

Let's break down the code:

- o `public class HelloWorld` defines a class named `HelloWorld`. In Java, every application must contain at least one class.

- o `public static void main(String[] args)` is the entry point of a Java application. When you run the program, the `main` method is executed first.
- o `System.out.println("Hello, World!");` is a command that outputs the text "Hello, World!" to the console.

4. **Running Your Java Program**

- o After writing the code, you can run it directly from your IDE by selecting the option to "Run" or by using the terminal/command prompt:

  - **In the terminal:** Navigate to the folder containing your `HelloWorld.java` file and compile it using the command:

    ```bash
    ```

    ```
    javac HelloWorld.java
    ```

  - After compiling, run the program using:

    ```bash
    ```

    ```
    java HelloWorld
    ```

- o You should see the following output:

  ```
  Hello, World!
  ```

21

Java Basics: Understanding the "Hello, World!" Program and Your First Steps

Now that you've written and executed your first Java program, let's take a deeper look at its structure to understand how everything works.

1. **Class Declaration**
   - o `public class HelloWorld` is where the class is defined. In Java, every application is made up of classes. A class is a blueprint for creating objects (instances), and methods are part of the class. The keyword `public` means that this class is accessible by other classes.

2. **The main Method**
   - o `public static void main(String[] args)` is a special method that serves as the entry point for a Java application. It's where the execution of your program begins. Here's what each part means:
     - `public`: The method is accessible from anywhere.
     - `static`: You can call this method without creating an instance of the class.

- • `void`: The method doesn't return any value.
- • `String[] args`: This parameter allows command-line arguments to be passed to the program.

3. **Outputting to the Console**
   - o `System.out.println("Hello, World!");` is a command used to display output to the console. `System.out` refers to the standard output stream, and `println` prints the message followed by a newline. If you want to print without a newline, you would use `print` instead of `println`.

Your Next Steps in Java Programming

At this point, you've taken your first steps into the world of Java programming. To continue your learning journey, here's what you should focus on next:

- • **Learning Variables and Data Types:** Understanding how to store and manipulate data.
- • **Exploring Control Flow:** Getting comfortable with decision-making structures like if-else and switch statements.

23

- **Practicing with Simple Programs:** Start building small applications that reinforce what you've learned so far.

With each new chapter, you'll continue to build on these fundamentals, gaining the skills needed to tackle more advanced topics in Java programming.

This chapter provides a solid foundation for any beginner, covering the essentials needed to start coding in Java. By the end of it, you'll be comfortable setting up your development environment and writing your first Java program. In the following chapters, we'll delve deeper into more complex topics, exploring the core concepts of Java in greater detail.

CHAPTER 2

UNDERSTANDING THE JAVA SYNTAX AND STRUCTURE

Basic Structure of Java Programs: From Classes to Methods

Java is an object-oriented programming (OOP) language, meaning everything in Java is encapsulated in classes and objects. When you write Java code, you follow a specific structure to organize and execute the program effectively. Let's break down the basic building blocks of a Java program.

1. **Class Declaration**

   o In Java, every program must have at least one class. A class is like a blueprint for objects that defines the attributes (fields) and behaviors (methods) of those objects.

   o The class keyword is used to define a class. A typical class definition looks like this:

```java

public class MyClass {
    // class content goes here
```

25

```
}
```

- o The `public` keyword specifies that the class is accessible from other classes, making it a common choice for the main class in most programs.

2. **The Main Method**
   - o Every Java application has an entry point where execution begins. This is the `main` method. It's a method within a class, and it must be declared exactly like this to run the program:

```java
public static void main(String[] args) {
    // program execution starts here
}
```

- o `public`: The method is accessible by any other class.
- o `static`: The method belongs to the class itself and not to any instance of the class.
- o `void`: The method doesn't return any value.
- o `String[] args`: This allows the program to receive input from the command line (though it's optional for basic programs).

Inside the `main` method is where you place your code that gets executed when the program runs.

3. **Methods**

   o Methods in Java define the behavior of objects and can be used to perform tasks or return values. Methods are declared inside a class, and their general structure looks like this:

java

```
public returnType methodName(parameters) {
    // method body
}
```

   o For example, here's a simple method that prints a message to the console:

java

```
public void printMessage() {
    System.out.println("Hello, Java!");
}
```

   o `void` means the method doesn't return a value.
   o `printMessage` is the name of the method.
   o The body of the method is enclosed in curly braces { }.

4. **Objects**

- o Once you have a class, you can create objects (instances of the class). Here's how you create an object from the MyClass class:

java

```
MyClass myObject = new MyClass();
```

- o This line creates an object of type MyClass and assigns it to the variable myObject.

Variables, Data Types, and Constants: A Guide to the Building Blocks of Java Programs

Variables are used to store data in a program. They are fundamental in Java, as they allow you to handle and manipulate data. Let's go over the essentials:

1. **Variables**
   - o A variable is essentially a container that holds data, and it must be declared with a specific data type. Here's how to declare a variable:

java

```
dataType variableName = value;
```

For example:

```java

int age = 25;
String name = "John";
```

- o `int` is the data type, indicating that the variable `age` will store integer values.
- o `String` is a data type that holds text.
- o The variable `name` stores the value `"John"`, a string.

2. **Data Types**
   - o **Primitive Data Types**: Java supports eight primitive data types, which are the most basic data types for storing simple values. They include:
     - `int`: Stores integer values (e.g., `-10`, `0`, `5`).
     - `double`: Stores decimal numbers (e.g., `3.14`, `-0.001`).
     - `char`: Stores single characters (e.g., `'a'`, `'B'`).
     - `boolean`: Stores true or false values.
     - `byte`, `short`, `long`: Variations of integer types that differ in size and range.

29

- **float**: A 32-bit floating-point number, useful for storing decimal values with less precision than `double`.
  - **Non-Primitive Data Types**: These include more complex types like `String`, arrays, and objects. For example:

```java
String message = "Hello, World!";
```

3. **Constants**

  - Constants are variables whose values cannot be changed once they are initialized. In Java, constants are declared using the `final` keyword. By convention, constants are written in uppercase letters with underscores separating words.

```java
final double PI = 3.14159;
final int MAX_USERS = 1000;
```

  - `final` ensures that the value of the variable cannot be modified after it's assigned.
  - This is useful when you have values that should remain constant throughout the program, such as

30

the value of Pi or the maximum number of users allowed.

The Importance of Semicolons, Braces, and Indentation

Java has a strict syntax that developers must follow, and the smallest mistakes, like missing semicolons, can cause errors. Let's break down the essentials:

1. **Semicolons**
   - In Java, most statements must end with a semicolon ;. It tells the Java compiler that the statement has ended. For example:

```java

int age = 25;   // semicolon marks the end
of the statement
System.out.println("Hello,  World!");   //
another semicolon here
```

   - Missing semicolons will lead to a compile-time error, so be sure to check them carefully.

2. **Braces**
   - Curly braces { } are used to define blocks of code. A block of code can be a method, class, loop, or

conditional statement. They group multiple statements into a single unit. For example:

```java
java

public class MyClass {
    public static void main(String[] args) {
        System.out.println("This is the start of the main method");
        if (age > 18) {
            System.out.println("You are an adult.");
        }
    }
}
```

- o In this example, the braces define the body of the `main` method and the `if` statement block.
- o Every class, method, and control flow statement in Java needs proper braces to define its boundaries.

3. **Indentation**
   - o Indentation helps make your code readable by visually indicating the hierarchy and structure of the program. While Java doesn't enforce indentation rules, proper formatting is essential for code maintainability.

o A common convention is to use 4 spaces per indentation level. For example:

```java

public class MyClass {
    public static void main(String[] args) {
        if (age > 18) {
            System.out.println("You are an adult.");
        }
    }
}
```

o Indentation makes the code more readable by clearly showing where blocks of code begin and end, which helps with debugging and collaboration.

Conclusion

In this chapter, you've learned the basic structure of Java programs, from classes to methods, and how Java programs are organized. You've also explored the core building blocks of any Java program, including variables, data types, constants, and the importance of semicolons, braces, and indentation.

With a solid understanding of these fundamental concepts, you're ready to tackle more complex topics in Java and start building your own programs. In the next chapters, we will explore control flow, loops, and more advanced features of Java programming.

CHAPTER 3

WRITING YOUR FIRST JAVA PROGRAM

A Step-by-Step Guide to Writing Your First Working Java Program

Now that you have an understanding of Java syntax and structure, it's time to dive into writing your very first working Java program. We'll go step-by-step to ensure you understand how everything fits together, from creating a class to running the program.

Let's write a simple Java program that asks the user for their name and age and then greets them with a message that includes their name and age.

1. **Create a Java File**
   o First, open your IDE or text editor and create a new Java file. Save it with the name `Greeting.java`. In Java, the filename must match the class name, so ensure the file is named exactly as the class within it.

2. **Write the Code**

Start by typing the following code into the file:

java

```
import java.util.Scanner;  // Import the
Scanner class for input

public class Greeting {
    public static void main(String[] args)
{
        // Create a Scanner object to get
user input
        Scanner    scanner    =    new
Scanner(System.in);

        // Ask the user for their name and
age
        System.out.print("Enter your name:
");
        String name = scanner.nextLine();
// Read the user's name

        System.out.print("Enter your age:
");
        int age = scanner.nextInt();   //
Read the user's age

        // Display a greeting message
        System.out.println("Hello,   "   +
name + "! You are " + age + " years old.");
```

```
        // Close the scanner object to free
up resources
        scanner.close();
    }
}
```

3. **Explanation of the Code**

   o **import java.util.Scanner;**: This line tells the program to import the Scanner class, which is part of Java's utility library and allows us to read input from the user.

   o **public class Greeting**: This defines a class named Greeting. The public keyword means this class can be accessed from anywhere.

   o **public static void main(String[] args)**: This is the main method where Java programs begin execution. Every Java application must have this method.

   o **Scanner scanner = new Scanner(System.in);**: This creates a new Scanner object, which will allow the program to read input from the user through the console (standard input).

   o **String name = scanner.nextLine();**: This line asks the user for their name and stores it as a String in the name variable.

37

- o `int age = scanner.nextInt();`: This line asks the user for their age and stores it as an integer in the `age` variable.

- o `System.out.println("Hello, " + name + "! You are " + age + " years old.");`: This line displays the greeting message, combining the user's name and age with a message.

- o `scanner.close();`: This is good practice to close the scanner object once you're done with it, freeing up system resources.

4. **Run the Program**

    - o To run your program, either use the "Run" button in your IDE or execute it through the terminal:

        - **In the terminal**: Navigate to the directory containing your `Greeting.java` file and run the following commands:

        ```bash
        ```

        ```
        javac Greeting.java      //
        Compile the program
        java Greeting      // Run the
        compiled program
        ```

    - o Once you run the program, it will ask for your name and age, then print a greeting message.

38

Example Output:

```yaml
yaml


Enter your name: John
Enter your age: 25
Hello, John! You are 25 years old.
```

Input/Output in Java: Using Scanner for User Input and System.out.println for Output

In Java, there are various ways to handle input and output (I/O). Let's break down how to use them effectively.

1. **Using the `Scanner` Class for Input**
   - The `Scanner` class is a part of Java's `java.util` package and is used for reading user input. In our program, we used the `nextLine()` method to read text and the `nextInt()` method to read integers.

   Common Scanner Methods:

   - `nextLine()`: Reads a whole line of text, including spaces.
   - `nextInt()`: Reads the next integer input from the user.

- o nextDouble(): Reads the next decimal number (double).
- o next(): Reads the next token (word) without spaces.

Example:

java

```
Scanner scanner = new Scanner(System.in);
String name = scanner.nextLine();  // Reads
a full line of input
int age = scanner.nextInt();        // Reads
an integer input
```

2. **Using System.out.println() for Output**

- o In Java, we use System.out.println() to output data to the console. The println() method prints a message followed by a newline, whereas System.out.print() does not append a newline.

Example:

java

```
System.out.println("Hello, World!");  //
Prints with a newline
```

40

```
System.out.print("Hello, ");          //
Prints without a newline
System.out.print("World!");           //
Prints "World!" on the same line
```

3. **Formatting Output**

    o   You can format your output to improve
        readability or display it in a specific style. Java
        offers ways to format strings using the
        `String.format()`   method   or
        `System.out.printf()`.

Example:

```
java

double price = 12.99;
System.out.printf("The price is $%.2f\n",
price);  // Prints: The price is $12.99
```

    o   This uses `%.2f` to format the floating-point
        number to two decimal places.

Debugging Tips and Common Errors for Beginners

When you first start programming in Java, you'll likely encounter
some common errors. Learning how to troubleshoot and debug

41

your programs is an essential skill. Here are some helpful tips for beginners:

1. **Syntax Errors**
   - These are the most common errors and occur when you violate the rules of Java syntax.
   - Common causes:
     - Missing semicolons at the end of statements.
     - Missing or mismatched braces `{}` for class, method, or control structures.
     - Misspelled keywords (e.g., `public` instead of `Public`).

   Solution: Carefully read the error message. Java will often tell you the line number and type of error. Fix the error and run the program again.

2. **Runtime Errors**
   - These errors occur while the program is running and typically cause the program to crash or behave unexpectedly.
   - Example: Dividing by zero, attempting to access an array index that doesn't exist, or running out of memory.

Solution: Use try-catch blocks to handle exceptions and print out informative error messages to understand the issue.

3. **Logical Errors**
   o These errors occur when the program runs without crashing, but it doesn't produce the expected result.
   o Example: You ask for the user's age, but the program prints the wrong result due to a mistake in the logic of your code.

Solution: Carefully check your program's logic and use `System.out.println()` to print intermediate values and verify the program's flow.

4. **Common Java Errors for Beginners**
   o **NullPointerException**: Occurs when you try to access or modify an object reference that is null.
      ▪ **Solution**: Always ensure an object is instantiated (i.e., `new`) before using it.
   o **ArrayIndexOutOfBoundsException**: Happens when you try to access an index in an array that doesn't exist.
      ▪ **Solution**: Make sure you are working within the bounds of the array.

5. **Using Debugging Tools**

43

o   Most IDEs (e.g., IntelliJ IDEA, Eclipse) offer built-in debugging tools. You can set breakpoints to pause the program's execution and inspect variable values at specific points in the code.

Conclusion

In this chapter, you've learned how to write and execute your first Java program, which takes user input and outputs a personalized message. You also gained an understanding of how to handle input and output in Java, using the `Scanner` class for reading user input and `System.out.println()` for displaying output.

Additionally, you've been introduced to common debugging tips and how to troubleshoot errors in your Java code. As you continue your Java journey, these skills will serve as the foundation for more complex programs.

In the next chapters, we will dive into control flow, loops, and other essential programming concepts.

Part 2

Diving Deeper into Java Basics

CHAPTER 4

CONTROL FLOW – MAKING DECISIONS IN JAVA

Understanding If-Else and Switch-Case Statements

Control flow in Java allows you to make decisions and execute certain blocks of code depending on specific conditions. The most commonly used control flow structures are `if-else` statements and `switch-case` statements.

1. **If-Else Statements**

   The `if` statement is the simplest form of decision-making in Java. It allows the program to execute a block of code if a given condition is true. If the condition is false, the program can execute an alternative block of code, which is specified using the `else` statement.

   Syntax:

```java

if (condition) {
    // Code to execute if condition is true
```

```
} else {
    // Code to execute if condition is
false
}
```

Example:

```
java

int age = 20;

if (age >= 18) {
    System.out.println("You     are     an
adult.");
} else {
    System.out.println("You     are     a
minor.");
}
```

In this example, if the age is 18 or greater, the program prints "You are an adult.". Otherwise, it prints "You are a minor.".

2. **If-Else If-Else Ladder**

Sometimes you need to check multiple conditions. In this case, you can chain if-else if-else statements to handle different scenarios.

47

Syntax:

```java
if (condition1) {
    // Code for condition1
} else if (condition2) {
    // Code for condition2
} else {
    // Code if all conditions fail
}
```

Example:

```java
int score = 85;

if (score >= 90) {
    System.out.println("Grade: A");
} else if (score >= 80) {
    System.out.println("Grade: B");
} else if (score >= 70) {
    System.out.println("Grade: C");
} else {
    System.out.println("Grade: F");
}
```

In this example, depending on the score variable, the program prints the corresponding grade.

3. **Switch-Case Statements**

A `switch` statement is useful when you have a single variable that can have multiple values, and you need to choose between them. It's an alternative to multiple `if-else if` conditions and can improve code readability.

Syntax:

```java

switch (expression) {
    case value1:
        // Code for value1
        break;
    case value2:
        // Code for value2
        break;
    default:
        // Code if no cases match
}
```

Example:

```java

int day = 3;
String dayName;
```

```
switch (day) {
    case 1:
        dayName = "Monday";
        break;
    case 2:
        dayName = "Tuesday";
        break;
    case 3:
        dayName = "Wednesday";
        break;
    default:
        dayName = "Invalid day";
        break;
}

System.out.println("Today    is:    "    +
dayName);
```

In this example, the switch statement checks the value of day and prints the corresponding day name. If no case matches, it prints "Invalid day".

Logical Operators and Conditionals: Combining Conditions for More Complex Logic

To make decisions more complex, we often need to combine multiple conditions. Java provides logical operators to achieve this.

1. **Logical AND (&&)**

   o The logical AND operator returns `true` only if both conditions are true.

   Example:

```java
int age = 25;
boolean hasLicense = true;

if (age >= 18 && hasLicense) {
    System.out.println("You are eligible to drive.");
} else {
    System.out.println("You are not eligible to drive.");
}
```

   This condition checks if both the `age` is greater than or equal to 18 and if the person has a driving license.

2. **Logical OR (||)**

   o The logical OR operator returns `true` if at least one of the conditions is true.

Example:

```java

int age = 16;
boolean hasPermission = true;

if (age >= 18 || hasPermission) {
    System.out.println("You are allowed to
attend the event.");
} else {
    System.out.println("You      are      not
allowed to attend the event.");
}
```

In this case, the condition checks if either the age is 18 or more, or if the person has permission. If either is true, they can attend.

3. **Logical NOT (!)**

   o   The logical NOT operator reverses the boolean value of a condition. If the condition is true, it becomes false, and vice versa.

Example:

```java

boolean isRaining = false;
```

```java
if (!isRaining) {
    System.out.println("It's not raining,
so you can go for a walk.");
} else {
    System.out.println("It's    raining,
better stay inside.");
}
```

The !isRaining condition checks if it's not raining. If the condition evaluates to true, it will print the message accordingly.

4. **Combining Logical Operators**

You can combine multiple logical operators to create more complex conditions.

Example:

java

```
int age = 20;
boolean isStudent = true;
boolean hasDiscount = false;

if ((age < 18 || isStudent) &&
!hasDiscount) {
    System.out.println("You are eligible
for a student discount.");
```

```
} else {
    System.out.println("You      are      not
eligible for a discount.");
}
```

This condition checks if either the person is under 18 or is a student, and at the same time, they don't have a discount. If this is true, the program prints that they are eligible for a student discount.

Practical Example: Building a Simple Number-Guessing Game

Let's combine what we've learned about control flow into a simple, practical application: a number-guessing game. In this game, the program will generate a random number, and the user will try to guess it.

1. **Write the Code**

   Here's a simple number-guessing game that uses an if-else structure and loops:

   java

   ```
   import java.util.Scanner;   // Import the
   Scanner class for user input
   ```

```java
import java.util.Random;    // Import the
Random class to generate random numbers

public class NumberGuessingGame {
    public static void main(String[] args)
{
        Scanner    scanner    =    new
Scanner(System.in);
        Random random = new Random();

        // Generate a random number between
1 and 100
        int        numberToGuess        =
random.nextInt(100) + 1;
        int userGuess = 0;
        int attempts = 0;

        System.out.println("Welcome to the
Number Guessing Game!");
        System.out.println("I        have
selected a number between 1 and 100. Try to
guess it!");

        // Game loop: Continue until the
user guesses the correct number
        while (userGuess != numberToGuess)
{
            System.out.print("Enter    your
guess: ");
```

```
            userGuess = scanner.nextInt();
// Read the user's guess
            attempts++;

            if (userGuess < numberToGuess)
{
                System.out.println("Too
low! Try again.");
            } else    if    (userGuess    >
numberToGuess) {
                System.out.println("Too
high! Try again.");
            } else {

System.out.println("Congratulations!
You've guessed the number in " + attempts
+ " attempts.");
            }
        }

        scanner.close();    // Close the
scanner
    }
}
```

2. **Explanation of the Code**

   o We use the `Random` class to generate a random
      number between 1 and 100.

- o The program prompts the user to guess the number. Each guess is compared using `if-else` statements.

- o The game loop continues until the user guesses the correct number. After each incorrect guess, the program provides feedback indicating whether the guess was too low or too high.

3. **Running the Game**

- o The user will be prompted to enter guesses until they correctly guess the number. The program will then display how many attempts it took to guess the correct number.

Example Output:

vbnet

```
Welcome to the Number Guessing Game!
I have selected a number between 1 and 100.
Try to guess it!
Enter your guess: 50
Too high! Try again.
Enter your guess: 25
Too low! Try again.
Enter your guess: 37
Congratulations! You've guessed the number
in 3 attempts.
```

Conclusion

In this chapter, you learned how to make decisions in Java using `if-else` and `switch-case` statements. We also explored logical operators like `&&`, `||`, and `!` to combine multiple conditions and make more complex decisions. By the end of the chapter, you applied your understanding of control flow by building a simple number-guessing game.

These fundamental concepts are key to writing interactive and dynamic Java programs. In the next chapters, we will explore loops and other advanced topics that will allow you to build even more powerful applications.

CHAPTER 5

LOOPS – REPEATING ACTIONS IN JAVA

Types of Loops in Java: For, While, and Do-While Loops

Loops in Java allow you to repeat a block of code multiple times, which is useful for tasks like processing items in a list, running simulations, or performing calculations. Java supports three main types of loops: **for**, **while**, and **do-while** loops. Each type has its own use case depending on the situation.

1. **For Loop**

   The `for` loop is typically used when you know beforehand how many times you want to repeat a block of code. It is especially useful for iterating over arrays or collections.

   Syntax:

   ```java
   java
   ```

59

```
for (initialization; condition; update) {
    // Code to be executed in each
iteration
}
```

Explanation:

- o **Initialization:** This step is executed once at the start of the loop. Typically, you declare and initialize a loop control variable (e.g., `int i = 0`).
- o **Condition:** This is the test that's evaluated before each iteration. If the condition is `true`, the loop executes. If it's `false`, the loop stops.
- o **Update:** After each iteration, this step is executed. It's used to modify the loop control variable (e.g., `i++`).

Example:

```
java

for (int i = 1; i <= 5; i++) {
    System.out.println("Iteration " + i);
}
```

This loop prints "Iteration 1", "Iteration 2", and so on, up to "Iteration 5".

2. While Loop

A `while` loop is used when you don't know in advance how many times the loop will run, but you want to continue looping as long as a certain condition is `true`.

Syntax:

```java

while (condition) {
    // Code to be executed while the condition is true
}
```

Explanation:

- o The loop will continue to execute as long as the condition remains `true`.
- o The condition is evaluated **before** each iteration. If the condition is false from the start, the loop will not execute even once.

Example:

```java
```

61

```
int i = 1;
while (i <= 5) {
    System.out.println("Iteration " + i);
    i++;    // Increment i to avoid an
infinite loop
}
```

This loop will print "Iteration 1" through "Iteration 5" and will stop when i exceeds 5.

---

3. Do-While Loop

The do-while loop is similar to the while loop, but with one key difference: the condition is evaluated **after** the loop's body is executed. This means that the loop will always execute at least once, even if the condition is false from the start.

Syntax:

```
java

do {
    // Code to be executed
} while (condition);
```

Explanation:

o   The body of the loop is executed first, and then the condition is checked.

o   If the condition is `true`, the loop repeats. If it's `false`, the loop exits.

Example:

```java

int i = 1;
do {
    System.out.println("Iteration " + i);
    i++;
} while (i <= 5);
```

This loop behaves similarly to the `while` loop but ensures that the code runs at least once, even if the condition were to be `false` on the first check.

When to Use Each Loop: Performance and Readability Considerations

Choosing the right loop depends on the specific task at hand, and understanding when to use each loop can enhance both the performance and readability of your code.

1. **For Loop**

- o **Use when:** You know the exact number of iterations beforehand or need to iterate over a range of numbers (such as arrays or collections).
- o **Example use cases:**
  - Iterating through an array.
  - Performing a fixed number of calculations.
- o **Performance considerations:** Since the `for` loop is typically used with a defined number of iterations, it's often the most efficient choice when the loop control variable is updated in a known manner.

2. **While Loop**
   - o **Use when:** The number of iterations is not known ahead of time and depends on some condition. The loop should continue until a specific condition becomes `false`.
   - o **Example use cases:**
     - Waiting for a user input or sensor data.
     - Looping through data until a specific condition is met.
   - o **Performance considerations:** The `while` loop is efficient when you don't know how many iterations are required, but make sure the condition will eventually become `false` to avoid infinite loops.

3. **Do-While Loop**

   o **Use when:** You need to ensure that the loop runs at least once before the condition is checked. This is useful when you want to prompt the user for input and ensure it happens at least once.

   o **Example use cases:**

     ▪ Asking the user for a valid input (e.g., re-prompting until a valid answer is given).

   o **Performance considerations:** The `do-while` loop is useful in scenarios where at least one iteration is required, even if the condition fails early. However, you should be cautious of infinite loops if the condition isn't correctly handled.

Practical Example: Building a Multiplication Table Using Loops

Let's combine what we've learned about loops by creating a simple program that generates a multiplication table. This will demonstrate how to use both `for` and `while` loops effectively.

1. **Task:** Write a program that generates a multiplication table for any given number (1 through 10).

2. **Solution Using For Loop**

```java
java

import java.util.Scanner;

public class MultiplicationTable {
    public static void main(String[] args) {
        Scanner scanner = new Scanner(System.in);

        // Ask the user for a number
        System.out.print("Enter a number to generate its multiplication table: ");
        int number = scanner.nextInt();

        // Generate multiplication table using a for loop
        System.out.println("Multiplication table for " + number + ":");
        for (int i = 1; i <= 10; i++) {
            System.out.println(number + " x " + i + " = " + (number * i));
        }

        scanner.close();    // Close the scanner
    }
}
```

Explanation:

- o The program asks the user for a number and then uses a `for` loop to print the multiplication table from 1 to 10.
- o The loop runs 10 times, each time printing a new multiplication fact.

Example Output:

```
css

Enter a number to generate its
multiplication table: 7
Multiplication table for 7:
7 x 1 = 7
7 x 2 = 14
7 x 3 = 21
7 x 4 = 28
7 x 5 = 35
7 x 6 = 42
7 x 7 = 49
7 x 8 = 56
7 x 9 = 63
7 x 10 = 70
```

3. **Solution Using While Loop**

Now let's use a `while` loop to achieve the same result:

```java
java

import java.util.Scanner;

public class MultiplicationTable {
    public static void main(String[] args)
{
        Scanner scanner = new
Scanner(System.in);

        // Ask the user for a number
        System.out.print("Enter a number
to generate its multiplication table: ");
        int number = scanner.nextInt();

        // Generate multiplication table
using a while loop

System.out.println("Multiplication table
for " + number + ":");
        int i = 1;
        while (i <= 10) {
            System.out.println(number + "
x " + i + " = " + (number * i));
            i++;  // Increment the counter
        }

        scanner.close();  // Close the
scanner
```

```
        }
    }
```

Explanation:

- o The `while` loop keeps running as long as `i` `<=` `10`. After each iteration, the value of `i` is incremented by 1.

Conclusion

In this chapter, we explored the different types of loops in Java: `for`, `while`, and `do-while`. We learned when to use each loop, considering performance and readability factors, and saw practical examples of how loops can simplify repetitive tasks. By building a multiplication table program, you gained hands-on experience in applying loops to real-world problems.

Loops are an essential tool in any Java developer's toolkit, enabling efficient repetition of tasks, whether you know the number of iterations upfront or need to loop until a condition is met.

In the next chapters, we will explore more advanced concepts such as arrays, methods, and object-oriented programming techniques that will build on the foundational knowledge of loops and control flow.

CHAPTER 6

ARRAYS – STORING MULTIPLE VALUES

Introduction to Arrays: Creating and Using Arrays in Java

In Java, arrays are used to store multiple values in a single variable. Arrays allow you to store collections of data efficiently and access elements using an index. When you have a group of related variables, rather than creating separate variables for each item, you can store them in an array.

What is an Array?

An array is a collection of variables, all of the same type, stored together in a contiguous block of memory. You can think of it as a list or collection where each item has a specific index, starting from 0.

How to Declare and Initialize an Array

1. **Declaring an Array:**

71

o To declare an array in Java, you specify the type of elements it will hold, followed by square brackets ([ ]) and the array name.

java

```
int[] numbers;
String[] names;
```

2. **Creating an Array:**

   o Once an array is declared, you need to create it using the new keyword, specifying the size of the array.

java

```
numbers = new int[5];  // Creates an array
of integers with 5 elements
names = new String[3]; // Creates an array
of strings with 3 elements
```

3. **Initializing an Array:**

   o You can initialize an array at the time of declaration by providing the values inside curly braces { }.

java

```
int[] numbers = {10, 20, 30, 40, 50};
```

72

```
String[] names = {"John", "Alice", "Bob"};
```

4. **Accessing Array Elements:**

   o You access array elements using the index number inside square brackets, starting from index 0.

```
java
```

```
System.out.println(numbers[0]); // Prints
the first element (10)
System.out.println(names[2]);    // Prints
the third element ("Bob")
```

5. **Modifying Array Elements:**

   o You can change the value of an array element by assigning a new value to the specific index.

```
java
```

```
numbers[1] = 25;   // Changes the second
element (20) to 25
```

Array Length

- You can determine the length of an array using the length property.

```
java
```

```
System.out.println(numbers.length);      //
Prints 5, the number of elements in the
array
```

Multidimensional Arrays: How and When to Use Them

While one-dimensional arrays are useful for storing a list of values, multidimensional arrays allow you to store more complex data structures, like tables or matrices. A multidimensional array is essentially an array of arrays.

1. **Declaring a Multidimensional Array:**
   o A common use of multidimensional arrays is for representing grids, tables, or matrices (like a chessboard or a student grades table).

   ```java
   ```

   ```java
   int[][]  matrix;    // Declare a two-
   dimensional array
   ```

2. **Creating a Multidimensional Array:**
   o You can create a multidimensional array in Java by specifying the size of each dimension.

   ```java
   ```

74

```
matrix = new int[3][4];  // Creates a 3x4
matrix (3 rows, 4 columns)
```

3. **Initializing a Multidimensional Array:**

   o You can also initialize a multidimensional array
   with values at the time of creation:

```
java
```

```
int[][] matrix = {
    {1, 2, 3, 4},
    {5, 6, 7, 8},
    {9, 10, 11, 12}
};
```

4. **Accessing Elements in Multidimensional Arrays:**

   o Just like with one-dimensional arrays, you use
   indices to access elements. For two-dimensional
   arrays, you use two indices: one for the row and
   one for the column.

```
java
```

```
System.out.println(matrix[0][0]);      //
Prints 1 (first element of the first row)
System.out.println(matrix[2][3]);      //
Prints 12 (last element of the third row)
```

5. **Example Use Case:**

o Multidimensional arrays are useful when working with grid-like data, such as a table of student grades across different subjects, or representing a chessboard.

Practical Example: Developing a Program That Sorts a List of Student Scores

Now that you understand the basics of arrays and multidimensional arrays, let's build a practical example where we'll use an array to store student scores and sort them in ascending order.

Problem:

We want to create a program that:

1. Takes the number of students and their scores as input.
2. Sorts the scores in ascending order.
3. Displays the sorted list of scores.

Solution:

We'll use a one-dimensional array to store the scores and the `Arrays.sort()` method to sort them. Here's how you can do it:

```java
java
```

```java
import java.util.Arrays;    // Import the Arrays
utility class
import java.util.Scanner;

public class SortStudentScores {
    public static void main(String[] args) {
        Scanner        scanner        =        new
Scanner(System.in);

        // Ask for the number of students
        System.out.print("Enter  the  number  of
students: ");
        int numStudents = scanner.nextInt();

        // Create an array to store the scores
        int[] scores = new int[numStudents];

        // Input student scores
        for (int i = 0; i < numStudents; i++) {
            System.out.print("Enter  score  for
student " + (i + 1) + ": ");
            scores[i] = scanner.nextInt();
        }

        // Sort the array in ascending order
        Arrays.sort(scores);

        // Display the sorted scores
```

```
System.out.println("Sorted scores:");
for (int score : scores) {
    System.out.println(score);
}

scanner.close();  // Close the scanner
    }
}
```

Explanation of the Code:

1. **Input the Number of Students:**
   o The program asks the user to enter the number of students, which is used to determine the size of the `scores` array.

2. **Input the Scores:**
   o A `for` loop is used to input the scores of each student. The scores are stored in the `scores` array.

3. **Sort the Array:**
   o The `Arrays.sort()` method is used to sort the scores in ascending order. It works in-place, meaning it sorts the array directly.

4. **Display the Sorted Scores:**
   o Another `for` loop is used to print the sorted list of scores.

Example Output:

yaml

```
Enter the number of students: 5
Enter score for student 1: 85
Enter score for student 2: 90
Enter score for student 3: 78
Enter score for student 4: 92
Enter score for student 5: 88
Sorted scores:
78
85
88
90
92
```

Conclusion

In this chapter, you learned how to store multiple values in arrays, including one-dimensional and multidimensional arrays. Arrays are a powerful tool in Java for organizing and managing data efficiently. We also covered practical use cases for multidimensional arrays and how to work with them.

You applied your knowledge by building a simple program that takes student scores, sorts them using an array, and displays the results. Sorting is just one of the many operations you can perform on arrays, and mastering arrays is a crucial step in becoming proficient in Java.

In the next chapters, we will explore methods, object-oriented programming, and more advanced data structures to expand your Java skills even further.

Part 3

Mastering Object-Oriented Programming (OOP) with Java

CHAPTER 7

INTRODUCTION TO OBJECT-ORIENTED PROGRAMMING (OOP)

What is OOP? Understanding the Four Pillars of OOP: Encapsulation, Abstraction, Inheritance, and Polymorphism

Object-Oriented Programming (OOP) is a programming paradigm that organizes software design around data, or objects, rather than functions and logic. In OOP, data is stored in the form of objects, which are instances of classes. Java is one of the most widely used object-oriented programming languages, and understanding its four main principles—**Encapsulation**, **Abstraction**, **Inheritance**, and **Polymorphism**—is key to becoming proficient in Java development.

1. Encapsulation: Protecting Data

Encapsulation is the process of bundling the data (fields) and methods (functions) that operate on the data into a single unit called a class. Additionally, it refers to restricting access to some of the object's components, typically by using access modifiers like private, protected, or public.

- **Why it matters**: Encapsulation helps protect an object's state by preventing direct access to its fields. Instead, access to data is controlled through methods (getters and setters).

Example of Encapsulation:

java

```
public class Car {
    // Private fields, cannot be accessed
directly from outside the class
    private String model;
    private int year;

    // Getter method for model
    public String getModel() {
        return model;
    }

    // Setter method for model
    public void setModel(String model) {
        this.model = model;
    }

    // Getter method for year
```

83

```java
public int getYear() {
    return year;
}

// Setter method for year
public void setYear(int year) {
    this.year = year;
}
}
```

In this example, the fields `model` and `year` are `private`, meaning they cannot be accessed directly from outside the class. To interact with these fields, we provide `getModel()` and `setModel()` methods (getters and setters), which allow controlled access to these fields.

---

2. Abstraction: Hiding Complexity

Abstraction is the concept of hiding the complex implementation details and showing only the essential features of the object. It allows a programmer to focus on high-level functionality without needing to understand the complex underlying logic.

- **Why it matters**: By abstracting away unnecessary details, you make your code easier to use, maintain, and scale.

In Java, abstraction can be achieved through:

- **Abstract Classes**: Classes that cannot be instantiated on their own, but must be subclassed.
- **Interfaces**: A contract for what methods a class should implement without specifying how they are implemented.

Example of Abstraction:

```java

abstract class Vehicle {
    // Abstract method (doesn't have a body)
    public abstract void start();

    // Regular method
    public void stop() {
        System.out.println("Vehicle stopped.");
    }
}

class Car extends Vehicle {
    // Providing implementation of the abstract
method
    public void start() {
        System.out.println("Car started.");
    }
}
```

Here, `Vehicle` is an abstract class that defines the structure of a `Vehicle` object. It declares the abstract method `start()`, but it doesn't implement it. The `Car` class extends `Vehicle` and provides an implementation for `start()`.

---

3. Inheritance: Reusing Code

Inheritance is a mechanism in OOP where a new class is derived from an existing class. The derived class (subclass) inherits the properties and behaviors (fields and methods) of the parent class (superclass). Inheritance allows for code reuse and creates a hierarchical relationship between classes.

- **Why it matters**: Inheritance promotes reusability and allows new classes to be created with minimal changes, leading to more efficient and maintainable code.

Example of Inheritance:

java

```java
class Animal {
    public void sound() {
        System.out.println("Some sound");
    }
}
```

```java
class Dog extends Animal {
    // Overriding the sound method
    public void sound() {
        System.out.println("Bark");
    }
}
```

In this example, the `Dog` class inherits from the `Animal` class, but it overrides the `sound()` method to provide its own implementation.

---

4. Polymorphism: Many Forms

Polymorphism is the ability of one object to take on many forms. In Java, polymorphism allows you to call methods on an object, even if the object's specific class isn't known at compile-time, by treating the object as an instance of a parent class or interface.

- **Why it matters**: Polymorphism allows for flexibility in your code and makes it easier to extend and maintain.

There are two types of polymorphism in Java:

- **Compile-time Polymorphism (Method Overloading)**: Occurs when you have multiple methods with the same name but different parameters.

87

- **Runtime Polymorphism (Method Overriding)**: Occurs when a subclass provides a specific implementation for a method that is already defined in the parent class.

Example of Polymorphism:

```java
java

class Shape {
    public void draw() {
        System.out.println("Drawing a shape");
    }
}

class Circle extends Shape {
    public void draw() {
        System.out.println("Drawing a circle");
    }
}

class Square extends Shape {
    public void draw() {
        System.out.println("Drawing a square");
    }
}

public class Test {
    public static void main(String[] args) {
        Shape shape = new Circle();  // Upcasting
```

88

```
        shape.draw();  // Calls the Circle's draw
method

        shape = new Square();  // Upcasting
        shape.draw();  // Calls the Square's draw
method
    }
}
```

In this example, both `Circle` and `Square` override the `draw()` method of the `Shape` class. The method that gets called depends on the object type, not the reference type, which is an example of runtime polymorphism.

Classes and Objects: Defining Classes and Creating Objects in Java

In Java, a **class** is a blueprint for creating objects, and an **object** is an instance of a class. A class defines the attributes (fields) and behaviors (methods) of an object, while an object represents a specific instance of that class with its own values for those attributes.

1. **Defining a Class**

89

    o A class is defined using the `class` keyword, followed by the class name. Inside the class, you define its fields and methods.

Example:

```java
java

class Car {
    String model;
    int year;

    // Constructor
    public Car(String model, int year) {
        this.model = model;
        this.year = year;
    }

    // Method
    public void displayDetails() {
        System.out.println("Model:    "    +
model);
        System.out.println("Year:     "    +
year);
    }
}
```

2. **Creating an Object**

o To create an object of a class, you use the new keyword followed by the constructor of the class.

Example:

```java

public class Main {
    public static void main(String[] args)
{
        // Creating an object of Car class
        Car   myCar   =   new   Car("Toyota
Corolla", 2020);

        // Calling the method on the object
        myCar.displayDetails();
    }
}
```

In this example, we create an object of the Car class named myCar and use the displayDetails() method to print its attributes.

Practical Example: A Simple Class to Model a Car

Let's apply what we've learned by creating a simple class to model a car. This class will include attributes like model and year, and methods like start() and stop() to simulate the car's actions.

1. **Create the Car Class**

```java

public class Car {
    // Fields (attributes)
    private String model;
    private int year;

    // Constructor
    public Car(String model, int year) {
        this.model = model;
        this.year = year;
    }

    // Method to simulate starting the car
    public void start() {
        System.out.println(model + " is starting.");
    }

    // Method to simulate stopping the car
    public void stop() {
        System.out.println(model + " is stopping.");
    }
```

```
    // Method to display car details
    public void displayDetails() {
        System.out.println("Model:    "    +
model);
        System.out.println("Year:     "    +
year);
    }
}
```

2. Create an Object and Use the Car Class

```java
public class TestCar {
    public static void main(String[] args)
{
        // Create a new Car object
        Car myCar = new Car("Honda Civic",
2021);

        // Call methods on the Car object
        myCar.displayDetails();
        myCar.start();
        myCar.stop();
    }
}
```

3. Example Output:

93

```vbnet
Model: Honda Civic
Year: 2021
Honda Civic is starting.
Honda Civic is stopping.
```

In this example, the `Car` class models the behavior of a car with `start()`, `stop()`, and `displayDetails()` methods. The object `myCar` represents a specific car with a model and year, demonstrating the power of OOP to model real-world entities.

Conclusion

In this chapter, you've learned the fundamentals of **Object-Oriented Programming (OOP)** in Java, including the four pillars: **Encapsulation**, **Abstraction**, **Inheritance**, and **Polymorphism**. You've explored how classes and objects are used to model real-world concepts, and you've implemented a simple `Car` class to put these concepts into practice.

Mastering OOP is essential for building scalable, maintainable, and reusable code in Java. As you continue learning, you'll dive deeper into more advanced OOP features, such as interfaces and abstract classes, that will further strengthen your understanding and ability to design powerful Java applications.

CHAPTER 8

METHODS AND CONSTRUCTORS IN JAVA

Understanding Methods: Declaration, Calling Methods, and Passing Arguments

Methods in Java are blocks of code that perform specific tasks and can be executed when called. Methods are essential for breaking down a large program into smaller, more manageable parts, which improves code readability, reusability, and maintainability.

1. Declaring a Method

A method is declared with the following syntax:

java

```
returnType methodName(parameters) {
    // Method body
}
```

- **returnType**: Specifies the type of value the method will return. If the method does not return anything, use void.

95

- **methodName**: The name of the method. By convention, method names are written in camelCase.
- **parameters**: A list of input values passed into the method. Parameters are optional; if a method does not need any input, you leave the parentheses empty.

Example:

java

```java
public int addNumbers(int a, int b) {
    return a + b;
}
```

In this example, the method addNumbers takes two integer parameters (a and b) and returns their sum.

2. Calling a Method

Once you declare a method, you can call it from another method, including the main method, to execute the code inside it.

Example:

java

```java
public class Calculator {
    public int addNumbers(int a, int b) {
        return a + b;
```

```
    }

    public static void main(String[] args) {
        Calculator calc = new Calculator();
        int result = calc.addNumbers(5, 10);   //
Calling the method
        System.out.println("Sum: " + result);
    }
}
```

In the `main` method, we created an object of the `Calculator` class (`calc`) and used it to call the `addNumbers` method. The method returns the sum of 5 and 10, and we print the result.

3. Passing Arguments to Methods

You can pass data into methods by providing arguments in the parentheses when calling the method. The type and number of arguments must match the method's parameters.

- **Passing by Value**: In Java, when you pass a primitive type (like `int`, `char`, `double`) to a method, it is passed by value, meaning the method gets a of the value.
- **Passing Objects**: When you pass an object, the method gets a reference to the object. This means the method can modify the object's properties.

Example with Primitive Types:

```java

public void printSquare(int number) {
    System.out.println("Square: " + (number *
number));
}

public static void main(String[] args) {
    Calculator calc = new Calculator();
    calc.printSquare(4);   // Passing the value 4
to the method
}
```

Example with Objects:

```java

class Person {
    String name;

    public Person(String name) {
        this.name = name;
    }
}

public void greetPerson(Person person) {
    System.out.println("Hello, " + person.name);
}

public static void main(String[] args) {
```

```
    Calculator calc = new Calculator();
    Person p = new Person("Alice");
    calc.greetPerson(p);    // Passing the object
p to the method
}
```

Constructors: Defining Constructors and Understanding the Difference Between Default and Parameterized Constructors

A **constructor** is a special type of method that is called when an object is instantiated. It is used to initialize objects of a class. Constructors share the same name as the class and do not have a return type.

There are two types of constructors in Java:

1. **Default Constructor**: This constructor is automatically provided by Java if no constructor is explicitly defined. It initializes object fields to default values (e.g., 0 for integers, null for objects).

2. **Parameterized Constructor**: This constructor allows you to pass arguments to the class when an object is created, enabling you to initialize the object with specific values.

1. Default Constructor

If you don't define any constructor, Java provides a default constructor for your class. This constructor does not take any parameters and initializes the object with default values.

Example of Default Constructor:

```java

class Car {
    String model;
    int year;

    // Default constructor
    public Car() {
        model = "Unknown";
        year = 0;
    }
}
```

In this case, the `Car` class has a default constructor that sets the `model` and `year` to "Unknown" and 0, respectively.

2. Parameterized Constructor

A parameterized constructor allows you to specify initial values for the fields when you create an object.

Example of Parameterized Constructor:

```java
java

class Car {
    String model;
    int year;

    // Parameterized constructor
    public Car(String model, int year) {
        this.model = model;
        this.year = year;
    }
}

public class Test {
    public static void main(String[] args) {
        // Using the parameterized constructor to
create an object
        Car myCar = new Car("Toyota", 2020);
        System.out.println("Model:        "      +
myCar.model);
        System.out.println("Year:         "      +
myCar.year);
    }
}
```

In this example, we have defined a parameterized constructor that takes two arguments, model and year, to initialize a Car object.

When creating a `Car` object in the `main` method, we pass values for these fields, and the constructor sets the object's attributes accordingly.

Practical Example: A Book Class with Methods to Display Details

Let's put all of this together by creating a `Book` class that demonstrates both methods and constructors. In this class, we will define a constructor to initialize the book details and methods to display those details.

Creating the Book Class:
java

```java
class Book {
    // Fields
    String title;
    String author;
    int yearPublished;

    // Constructor to initialize the book object
    public Book(String title, String author, int
yearPublished) {
        this.title = title;
        this.author = author;
        this.yearPublished = yearPublished;
```

```
    }

    // Method to display book details
    public void displayDetails() {
        System.out.println("Title: " + title);
        System.out.println("Author: " + author);
        System.out.println("Year Published: " +
yearPublished);
    }

    // Method to update the year of publication
    public void updateYearPublished(int newYear)
{
        yearPublished = newYear;
        System.out.println("Year        Published
updated to: " + yearPublished);
    }
}

public class TestBook {
    public static void main(String[] args) {
        // Creating a Book object using the
parameterized constructor
        Book myBook = new Book("1984", "George
Orwell", 1949);

        // Displaying book details
        myBook.displayDetails();
```

```
        // Updating the year of publication
        myBook.updateYearPublished(1950);

        // Displaying the updated details
        myBook.displayDetails();
    }
}
```

Explanation of the Code:

1. **Book Class**:
    - The `Book` class has three fields: `title`, `author`, and `yearPublished`.
    - The constructor `public Book(String title, String author, int yearPublished)` initializes these fields when a `Book` object is created.
    - The method `displayDetails()` displays the details of the book.
    - The method `updateYearPublished(int newYear)` allows you to change the year of publication and prints the updated year.

2. **TestBook Class**:
    - In the `TestBook` class, we create a `Book` object using the parameterized constructor and call the methods to display and update the book's details.

Example Output:

```yaml
Title: 1984
Author: George Orwell
Year Published: 1949
Year Published updated to: 1950
Title: 1984
Author: George Orwell
Year Published: 1950
```

In this practical example, we used both a **parameterized constructor** to initialize a `Book` object and **methods** to interact with it. By calling the `displayDetails()` method, we could output the book's information, and the `updateYearPublished()` method allowed us to modify the book's year of publication.

Conclusion

In this chapter, you've learned how to define and use methods and constructors in Java. You saw how methods help break down complex tasks into manageable units of work, while constructors allow you to initialize objects with specific values. Through the practical example of the `Book` class, you applied these concepts to build an object-oriented model that is reusable and maintainable.

In the next chapters, we'll explore more advanced topics in Java, including inheritance, polymorphism, and other key object-oriented programming concepts. These concepts will further strengthen your ability to build scalable and efficient Java applications.

CHAPTER 9

INHERITANCE – REUSING CODE IN JAVA

What is Inheritance? How Inheritance Allows for Code Reuse and the Relationship Between Parent and Child Classes

Inheritance is one of the four fundamental pillars of Object-Oriented Programming (OOP). It allows one class (the **child** or **subclass**) to inherit fields and methods from another class (the **parent** or **superclass**). The child class can then add its own methods and fields or override the methods of the parent class. Inheritance promotes **code reuse**, meaning you don't have to rewrite the same functionality in multiple places.

1. The Basics of Inheritance

In Java, inheritance is implemented using the `extends` keyword. A subclass inherits all the **non-private** members (fields and methods) from its superclass. The subclass can then use or modify the inherited members.

Syntax:

107

```java
java

class ChildClass extends ParentClass {
    // Additional fields and methods specific to
the child class
}
```

2. Benefits of Inheritance

- **Code Reusability**: Inheritance allows you to reuse code from the parent class in the child class without rewriting it.

- **Hierarchical Classification**: Inheritance establishes a relationship between classes, making it easier to understand and model real-world relationships (e.g., a dog is an animal).

- **Extensibility**: Child classes can extend the functionality of the parent class, allowing for flexible and scalable designs.

Overriding Methods: Understanding Method Overriding in Java

Method overriding occurs when a subclass provides its own specific implementation of a method that is already defined in its superclass. This is useful when a subclass needs to modify or

108

completely replace the behavior of a method inherited from the parent class.

1. Rules of Method Overriding

- **Same Method Signature**: The method in the subclass must have the same name, return type, and parameter list as the method in the parent class.
- **Access Modifier**: The overridden method in the subclass cannot have a more restrictive access level than the method in the superclass. For example, if the parent class method is `public`, the child class method must also be `public`.
- **@Override Annotation**: While not required, it's good practice to use the `@Override` annotation to make the intention clear and to let the compiler check for potential issues.

Example of Method Overriding:

java

```java
class Animal {
    public void sound() {
        System.out.println("Some generic animal
sound");
    }
}
```

```java
class Dog extends Animal {
    @Override
    public void sound() {
        System.out.println("Bark");
    }
}


public class Test {
    public static void main(String[] args) {
        Animal myAnimal = new Animal();
        myAnimal.sound();     // Output: Some generic animal sound

        Dog myDog = new Dog();
        myDog.sound();  // Output: Bark
    }
}
```

In this example:

- The `Dog` class overrides the `sound()` method of the `Animal` class to provide a more specific implementation.
- When we call `myDog.sound()`, it outputs `"Bark"`, which is the overridden version of the `sound()` method.

2. Overloading vs. Overriding

- **Method Overloading**: Occurs when a class has multiple methods with the same name but different parameters (different number or type of arguments).
- **Method Overriding**: Occurs when a subclass provides its own version of a method that is already defined in the parent class with the same signature.

Practical Example: Creating a Hierarchy of Animal and Dog Classes

Let's now apply inheritance and method overriding by creating a simple hierarchy of animal classes. We'll define a parent class Animal and a child class Dog, and then override a method to make the dog bark.

1. **Define the Parent Class (Animal)**: This class will represent a generic animal with a sound() method.

```java

class Animal {
    // Fields (attributes)
    String name;
```

111

```
    // Constructor to initialize the
animal's name
    public Animal(String name) {
        this.name = name;
    }

    // Method to simulate the sound of an
animal
    public void sound() {
        System.out.println("This     animal
makes a sound.");
    }

    // Method to display the animal's name
    public void displayName() {
        System.out.println("Animal's name:
" + name);
    }
}
```

2. **Define the Child Class (Dog)**: The Dog class extends the Animal class and overrides the sound() method to provide a more specific implementation for dogs.

java

```
class Dog extends Animal {
    // Constructor for Dog class
    public Dog(String name) {
```

112

```
        super(name);   // Call the parent
constructor to initialize the name
    }

    // Overriding the sound method
    @Override
    public void sound() {
        System.out.println("The         dog
barks.");
    }

    // Method to display dog-specific
information
    public void wagTail() {
        System.out.println("The  dog  wags
its tail.");
    }
}
```

3. **Using the Animal and Dog Classes**: In the `main` method, we will create objects of both the `Animal` and `Dog` classes and call their methods to demonstrate inheritance and method overriding.

```
java

public class TestAnimal {
    public static void main(String[] args)
    {
```

```
        // Create an Animal object
        Animal    myAnimal    =    new
Animal("Generic Animal");
        myAnimal.displayName();
        myAnimal.sound();    // Calls the
Animal's sound method

        // Create a Dog object
        Dog myDog = new Dog("Buddy");
        myDog.displayName();
        myDog.sound();    // Calls the
overridden sound method in Dog
        myDog.wagTail();    // Calls the
Dog's unique method
    }
}
```

Explanation of the Code:

- **Animal Class**:
  - The `Animal` class has a `name` field and a `sound()` method that outputs a generic message. It also has a `displayName()` method to print the animal's name.
- **Dog Class**:
  - The `Dog` class extends `Animal` and overrides the `sound()` method to specify that dogs bark.
  - It also introduces a new method, `wagTail()`, which is unique to the `Dog` class.

114

- **TestAnimal Class**:
  - In the `main` method, we create both an `Animal` object and a `Dog` object.
  - We call the `sound()` method on both objects. The `Animal` object calls the base `sound()` method, while the `Dog` object calls the overridden `sound()` method.
  - The `Dog` object also calls the `wagTail()` method, which is unique to the `Dog` class.

Example Output:

```bash

Animal's name: Generic Animal
This animal makes a sound.
Animal's name: Buddy
The dog barks.
The dog wags its tail.
```

Conclusion

In this chapter, you've learned about **inheritance**, one of the most powerful concepts in Java that allows for code reuse and creating hierarchical relationships between classes. You also learned about **method overriding**, which allows subclasses to provide their own implementation of methods from the parent class.

By creating a simple hierarchy with the `Animal` and `Dog` classes, you saw how inheritance works in practice, and how you can extend and modify the behavior of parent classes in subclasses.

Inheritance and method overriding are essential concepts in object-oriented design, enabling more flexible and reusable code. In the next chapters, we'll dive deeper into other object-oriented principles, such as **polymorphism** and **abstract classes**, to enhance your Java programming skills further.

CHAPTER 10

POLYMORPHISM AND ABSTRACTION

Polymorphism: The Power of Using Objects of Different Types Interchangeably

Polymorphism is one of the key features of object-oriented programming that allows an object of a subclass to be treated as an object of its superclass. The word "polymorphism" comes from Greek and means "many forms." In programming, it refers to the ability to use different classes in a similar way, through the same interface, allowing for greater flexibility and scalability.

There are two types of polymorphism in Java:

1. **Compile-time Polymorphism (Method Overloading)**: Occurs when you have multiple methods with the same name but different parameter types or numbers.

2. **Runtime Polymorphism (Method Overriding)**: Occurs when a subclass provides a specific implementation of a method that is already defined in the superclass.

1. Compile-time Polymorphism (Method Overloading)

Method overloading occurs when a class has multiple methods with the same name but different parameters. The compiler determines which method to call based on the number and type of arguments passed.

Example of Method Overloading:

```java
class Calculator {
    // Method to add two integers
    public int add(int a, int b) {
        return a + b;
    }

    // Method to add three integers
    public int add(int a, int b, int c) {
        return a + b + c;
    }

    // Method to add two doubles
    public double add(double a, double b) {
        return a + b;
    }
}

public class Test {
```

```
public static void main(String[] args) {
    Calculator calc = new Calculator();

    // Calling overloaded methods
    System.out.println("Sum of two integers:
" + calc.add(5, 10));
    System.out.println("Sum      of      three
integers: " + calc.add(5, 10, 15));
    System.out.println("Sum of two doubles:
" + calc.add(5.5, 10.5));
    }
}
```

In this example:

- The `add` method is overloaded with different parameter types and counts.
- Depending on the arguments passed, the appropriate version of the `add` method is called.

2. Runtime Polymorphism (Method Overriding)

Runtime polymorphism, or method overriding, occurs when a subclass provides its own specific implementation of a method that is already defined in its superclass. This is typically achieved using inheritance and the `@Override` annotation.

Example of Method Overriding:

```
java

class Animal {
    public void sound() {
        System.out.println("Some generic animal
sound");
    }
}

class Dog extends Animal {
    @Override
    public void sound() {
        System.out.println("Bark");
    }
}

class Cat extends Animal {
    @Override
    public void sound() {
        System.out.println("Meow");
    }
}

public class Test {
    public static void main(String[] args) {
        Animal myAnimal = new Animal();
        Animal myDog = new Dog();
        Animal myCat = new Cat();
```

```
    myAnimal.sound();      // Outputs: Some
generic animal sound
    myDog.sound();      // Outputs: Bark
    myCat.sound();      // Outputs: Meow
    }
}
```

In this example:

- Both `Dog` and `Cat` classes override the `sound()` method from the `Animal` class.

- The variable `myDog` and `myCat` are references of type `Animal`, but they refer to objects of type `Dog` and `Cat`, respectively.

- At runtime, the `sound()` method corresponding to the actual object type (not the reference type) is invoked, demonstrating polymorphism.

Abstraction: Hiding Complexity and Providing Simple Interfaces

Abstraction is the process of hiding the complex implementation details of a system while exposing only the essential features or functionality. In Java, abstraction is achieved through:

- **Abstract Classes**

121

- **Interfaces**

Abstraction allows you to provide a simple interface for interacting with objects, while the internal implementation can change without affecting the users of the class or interface.

1. Abstract Classes

An abstract class is a class that cannot be instantiated on its own and must be subclassed. It can have both abstract methods (methods without a body) and concrete methods (methods with a body). Subclasses are required to provide implementations for the abstract methods.

Example of Abstract Class:

java

```java
abstract class Shape {
    // Abstract method
    public abstract void draw();

    // Concrete method
    public void displayColor() {
        System.out.println("Displaying color");
    }
}

class Circle extends Shape {
```

122

```java
    @Override
    public void draw() {
        System.out.println("Drawing a circle");
    }
}


class Rectangle extends Shape {
    @Override
    public void draw() {
        System.out.println("Drawing          a
rectangle");
    }
}


public class Test {
    public static void main(String[] args) {
        Shape circle = new Circle();
        Shape rectangle = new Rectangle();

        circle.draw();        // Outputs: Drawing
a circle
        rectangle.draw();     // Outputs: Drawing
a rectangle
    }
}
```

In this example:

- Shape is an abstract class with an abstract method draw() and a concrete method displayColor().
- Both Circle and Rectangle classes extend Shape and implement the draw() method.

2. Interfaces

An interface is similar to an abstract class, but it can only contain abstract methods (unless using Java 8+ default methods). A class can implement multiple interfaces, whereas it can only extend one class.

Example of Interface:

java

```java
interface PaymentMethod {
    void pay(int amount);  // Abstract method
}

class CreditCard implements PaymentMethod {
    @Override
    public void pay(int amount) {
        System.out.println("Paying " + amount +
" using Credit Card.");
    }
}

class PayPal implements PaymentMethod {
```

```java
    @Override
    public void pay(int amount) {
        System.out.println("Paying " + amount +
" using PayPal.");
    }
}


public class Test {
    public static void main(String[] args) {
        PaymentMethod    myPayment    =    new
CreditCard();
        myPayment.pay(100);   // Outputs: Paying
100 using Credit Card.

        myPayment = new PayPal();
        myPayment.pay(50);    // Outputs: Paying
50 using PayPal.
    }
}
```

In this example:

- `PaymentMethod` is an interface with an abstract method `pay()`.
- Both `CreditCard` and `PayPal` classes implement the `PaymentMethod` interface, providing their own versions of the `pay()` method.

Practical Example: Designing a Payment System with Different Payment Methods

Let's put together everything we've learned about **polymorphism** and **abstraction** by designing a simple payment system where users can pay using different payment methods like **Credit Card**, **PayPal**, or **Cash**.

1. **Define the Payment Interface:** The `PaymentMethod` interface will declare a `pay()` method.

   java

   ```java
   interface PaymentMethod {
       void pay(int amount);
   }
   ```

2. **Implement Different Payment Methods:** We'll implement the `PaymentMethod` interface for different types of payment methods, such as `CreditCard`, `PayPal`, and `Cash`.

   java

   ```java
   class CreditCard implements PaymentMethod
   {
       @Override
       public void pay(int amount) {
   ```

```java
        System.out.println("Paying    " +
amount + " using Credit Card.");
    }
}


class PayPal implements PaymentMethod {
    @Override
    public void pay(int amount) {
        System.out.println("Paying    " +
amount + " using PayPal.");
    }
}


class Cash implements PaymentMethod {
    @Override
    public void pay(int amount) {
        System.out.println("Paying    " +
amount + " using Cash.");
    }
}
```

3. **Main Program to Test Polymorphism:** In the main method, we will create objects of different payment methods and use polymorphism to pay using the desired method.

```java
java


public class PaymentSystem {
```

```
public static void main(String[] args)
{
        PaymentMethod    payment    =    new
CreditCard();
        payment.pay(100);      //  Outputs:
Paying 100 using Credit Card.

        payment = new PayPal();
        payment.pay(50);      //  Outputs:
Paying 50 using PayPal.

        payment = new Cash();
        payment.pay(20);      //  Outputs:
Paying 20 using Cash.
    }
}
```

Explanation of the Code:

- **PaymentMethod Interface**: The interface defines a common method pay(int amount) that all payment methods must implement.
- **Polymorphism**: We use polymorphism to assign different PaymentMethod objects (like CreditCard, PayPal, and Cash) to the payment reference. Regardless of the object type, we can call the pay() method, and the appropriate method is invoked at runtime.

128

- **Abstraction**: The internal details of how each payment method works are hidden. The user only interacts with the `pay()` method through the `PaymentMethod` interface, without needing to understand the details of each payment method.

Conclusion

In this chapter, you learned about **polymorphism** and **abstraction** in Java. Polymorphism allows you to treat different objects of different types in a similar way, making your code more flexible and extensible. Abstraction hides the complexity of a system and provides a simple interface for interacting with objects, improving code readability and maintainability.

We demonstrated these concepts through the creation of a simple payment system with multiple payment methods. By using interfaces and method overriding, we designed a flexible and scalable solution that can easily be extended to support additional payment methods.

In the next chapters, we'll dive deeper into advanced OOP concepts like **abstract classes**, **interfaces**, and **exception handling**, to further enhance your Java programming skills.

CHAPTER 11

INTERFACES AND ABSTRACT CLASSES

Interfaces vs Abstract Classes: Understanding the Differences and When to Use Them

In Java, both **interfaces** and **abstract classes** are used to achieve abstraction, but they serve different purposes. Understanding when to use an interface and when to use an abstract class is crucial for effective object-oriented design. Let's break down the differences between the two and their appropriate use cases.

1. What is an Interface?

An **interface** is a contract that defines a set of abstract methods (methods without implementation) that a class must implement. An interface cannot have any implementation (though default methods were introduced in Java 8, which allow method implementations in interfaces).

Key Points about Interfaces:

- **Method Signature**: An interface defines **only method signatures**. It doesn't provide any implementation.
- **Multiple Inheritance**: A class can implement multiple interfaces, which allows for multiple inheritance of types.
- **Implementation**: A class that implements an interface must provide an implementation for all methods declared in the interface (unless the class is abstract).

Syntax to Define an Interface:

```java
interface InterfaceName {
    // Abstract methods
    void method1();
    void method2();
}
```

Example:

```java
interface Drawable {
    void draw();  // Abstract method
}

class Circle implements Drawable {
    @Override
    public void draw() {
```

```
        System.out.println("Drawing a circle.");
    }
}


class Rectangle implements Drawable {
    @Override
    public void draw() {
        System.out.println("Drawing          a
rectangle.");
    }
}
```

In this example, Drawable is an interface, and both Circle and Rectangle classes implement the draw() method.

2. What is an Abstract Class?

An **abstract class** is a class that cannot be instantiated on its own and can have both **abstract methods** (without implementation) and **concrete methods** (with implementation). It allows for code reuse and provides a common base for subclasses to extend and implement additional functionality.

Key Points about Abstract Classes:

- **Can Have Both Abstract and Concrete Methods**: Abstract classes can provide some method implementations, and subclasses can override these methods.

132

- **Single Inheritance**: A class can only extend one abstract class because Java doesn't support multiple inheritance for classes.
- **Constructor**: Abstract classes can have constructors, which can be invoked by subclasses.

Syntax to Define an Abstract Class:

java

```
abstract class AbstractClass {
    // Abstract method
    abstract void method1();

    // Concrete method
    void method2() {
        System.out.println("This  is  a  concrete
method.");
    }
}
```

Example:

java

```
abstract class Animal {
    abstract void sound();

    void eat() {
```

```
        System.out.println("This    animal    eats
food.");
    }
}


class Dog extends Animal {
    @Override
    void sound() {
        System.out.println("Bark");
    }
}
```

In this example, the `Animal` class is abstract and contains both an abstract method (`sound()`) and a concrete method (`eat()`). The `Dog` class extends `Animal` and provides its own implementation of the `sound()` method.

3. Key Differences Between Interfaces and Abstract Classes

Feature	Interface	Abstract Class
Purpose	Defines a contract for classes to implement	Provides a common base for classes

Feature	Interface	Abstract Class
Method Implementation	Methods cannot have a body (except default methods)	Can have both abstract and concrete methods
Inheritance	A class can implement multiple interfaces	A class can extend only one abstract class
Fields	Can only have `static` `final` fields (constants)	Can have instance variables and constants
Constructor	Cannot have constructors	Can have constructors
Access Modifiers	Methods are `public` by default	Can have any access modifier (e.g., `protected`, `private`)

When to Use an Interface:

- When you need to define a contract that must be followed by multiple classes.

- When you want to provide a common set of methods across multiple classes, but the classes don't need to share common implementation.
- When you need multiple inheritance (a class can implement multiple interfaces).

When to Use an Abstract Class:

- When you want to provide some common functionality to subclasses but also want to enforce certain methods to be implemented by subclasses.
- When the classes have a clear hierarchical relationship and some common behavior can be inherited.
- When you need constructors to initialize fields in a class hierarchy.

Practical Example: Implementing an Interface for a Drawable Object

Let's create an interface `Drawable` with a `draw()` method, and then implement this interface in different classes such as `Circle`, `Rectangle`, and `Triangle`. These classes will provide their own specific implementation of the `draw()` method, demonstrating polymorphism and abstraction.

136

Step 1: Define the `Drawable` *Interface*

java

```java
interface Drawable {
    void draw();   // Abstract method to be implemented by any class that implements this interface
}
```

Step 2: Implement the `Drawable` *Interface in Different Classes*

java

```java
class Circle implements Drawable {
    @Override
    public void draw() {
        System.out.println("Drawing a circle.");
    }
}


class Rectangle implements Drawable {
    @Override
    public void draw() {
        System.out.println("Drawing                a rectangle.");
    }
}


class Triangle implements Drawable {
    @Override
    public void draw() {
```

137

```
        System.out.println("Drawing        a
triangle.");
    }
}
```

Here, each class (`Circle`, `Rectangle`, `Triangle`) implements the `draw()` method, providing its own implementation for drawing the respective shapes.

Step 3: Test the Drawable Objects

Now, in the `main` method, we will create instances of the `Circle`, `Rectangle`, and `Triangle` classes and call the `draw()` method on each of them using polymorphism.

java

```
public class TestDrawable {
    public static void main(String[] args) {
        Drawable circle = new Circle();        //
Polymorphism in action
        Drawable rectangle = new Rectangle();
        Drawable triangle = new Triangle();

        circle.draw();        // Outputs: Drawing a
circle.
        rectangle.draw();  // Outputs: Drawing a
rectangle.
```

```
        triangle.draw();    // Outputs: Drawing a
triangle.
    }
}
```

In this example:

- The `Drawable` interface provides a blueprint for all shapes that can be drawn.
- Each shape class (`Circle, Rectangle, Triangle`) implements the `draw()` method differently, which shows polymorphism in action.
- The `main` method demonstrates how objects of different types (`Circle, Rectangle,` and `Triangle`) can be treated uniformly as `Drawable` objects, and their respective `draw()` methods are called.

Example Output:

css

```
Drawing a circle.
Drawing a rectangle.
Drawing a triangle.
```

Conclusion

In this chapter, we explored the concepts of **interfaces** and **abstract classes** in Java. You learned how interfaces define a contract for classes to follow, while abstract classes provide a base for classes to build upon with both abstract and concrete methods. Understanding when and how to use interfaces and abstract classes is crucial for creating scalable and maintainable object-oriented systems.

Through the practical example of the `Drawable` interface, you saw how polymorphism and abstraction can be used to provide a common interface for different objects while allowing each object to define its own specific behavior.

In the next chapters, we will continue to expand on these concepts and dive deeper into more advanced object-oriented techniques, such as working with collections, exception handling, and file input/output in Java.

Part 4

Advanced Java Concepts

CHAPTER 12

EXCEPTION HANDLING IN JAVA

Understanding Exceptions: What They Are and How They Affect Your Program

In Java, an **exception** is an event that disrupts the normal flow of execution in a program. It occurs when an abnormal condition or error arises, such as trying to divide by zero, accessing a file that doesn't exist, or attempting to use a null reference.

When an exception occurs, it typically causes the program to stop unless the exception is handled properly. Proper exception handling is essential to prevent your application from crashing unexpectedly and to provide meaningful error messages to users or developers.

Types of Exceptions

Java exceptions are categorized into two main types:

1. **Checked Exceptions**: These exceptions are checked at compile-time. They must be either caught or declared in the method signature. Examples include `IOException`, `SQLException`, and `FileNotFoundException`.

2. **Unchecked Exceptions**: These exceptions are not checked at compile-time, and they extend the `RuntimeException` class. Examples include `NullPointerException`, `ArithmeticException`, and `ArrayIndexOutOfBoundsException`.

How Exceptions Affect Your Program

When an exception occurs, Java creates an **exception object** that contains information about the error, including:

- The type of exception.
- A message describing the exception.
- The stack trace, which shows the method calls that led to the exception.

If the exception is not handled, the program will terminate and display the stack trace. However, by catching and handling exceptions, you can ensure that the program continues running or provides a user-friendly error message.

Try-Catch-Finally: Handling Exceptions to Ensure Smooth Execution

Java provides a robust mechanism for exception handling using the `try`, `catch`, and `finally` blocks. Let's break down how each block works:

1. **Try Block**:
   - The code that may throw an exception is placed inside the `try` block.
   - If an exception occurs, the flow of control moves to the corresponding `catch` block (if one exists).

2. **Catch Block**:
   - The `catch` block is used to handle the exception. It must follow the `try` block.
   - You can catch specific types of exceptions, allowing you to handle different errors in different ways.

3. **Finally Block**:
   - The `finally` block is optional but useful. It contains code that will always execute, regardless of whether an exception is thrown or not.
   - It is typically used for cleanup operations like closing files, releasing resources, or resetting variables.

Syntax:

```java
java
```

```
try {
    // Code that may throw an exception
} catch (ExceptionType1 e1) {
    // Handle exception of type ExceptionType1
} catch (ExceptionType2 e2) {
    // Handle exception of type ExceptionType2
} finally {
    // Code that will run whether an exception
occurs or not
}
```

Example: Using Try-Catch-Finally

java

```
public class ExceptionExample {
    public static void main(String[] args) {
        try {
            int result = 10 / 0;  // Division by
zero (ArithmeticException)
            System.out.println("Result:    "    +
result);
        } catch (ArithmeticException e) {
            System.out.println("Error:    Cannot
divide by zero.");
        } finally {
            System.out.println("This will always
execute.");
        }
    }
}
```

In this example:

- The `try` block attempts to divide 10 by zero, which will throw an `ArithmeticException`.
- The `catch` block handles the exception by printing a custom error message.
- The `finally` block executes regardless of whether an exception occurred, ensuring that the program doesn't leave resources in an inconsistent state.

Output:

pgsql

```
Error: Cannot divide by zero.
This will always execute.
```

Practical Example: Handling File Reading Exceptions with Custom Error Messages

Handling file-related exceptions is common in Java programs, especially when dealing with file I/O (input/output) operations. In this example, we'll create a program that attempts to read a file and handle possible exceptions, such as the file not being found or issues reading from the file.

146

Step 1: Create a Text File (Example: `example.txt`)

For this example, let's assume we have a text file named `example.txt` with the following content:

```
kotlin
```

```
Hello, this is a test file.
Welcome to Java Exception Handling.
```

Step 2: Write the Java Code to Read the File

We'll write a program that reads the content of this file, handling potential exceptions like the file not existing or being unreadable.

```java
java

import java.io.BufferedReader;
import java.io.FileNotFoundException;
import java.io.FileReader;
import java.io.IOException;

public class FileReaderExample {
    public static void main(String[] args) {
        BufferedReader reader = null;

        try {
            // Attempt to open the file
            reader  =  new  BufferedReader(new
FileReader("example.txt"));
```

147

```
        // Read and print the file content
line by line
        String line;
        while ((line = reader.readLine()) !=
null) {
            System.out.println(line);
        }
    } catch (FileNotFoundException e) {
        // Handle the case when the file is
not found
        System.out.println("Error: The file
was not found.");
    } catch (IOException e) {
        // Handle other I/O errors
        System.out.println("Error: There was
an issue reading the file.");
    } finally {
        // Ensure the BufferedReader is
closed, whether an exception occurs or not
        try {
            if (reader != null) {
                reader.close();
            }
        } catch (IOException e) {
            System.out.println("Error:
Failed to close the file reader.");
        }
    }
```

```
    }
}
```

Explanation of the Code:

1. **BufferedReader**: We use a `BufferedReader` to read the file line by line. This is more efficient than reading the file character by character.

2. **Try Block**: The file is opened inside the `try` block using `FileReader`, and each line is printed out.

3. **Catch Blocks**:
   - The first `catch` block handles the `FileNotFoundException`, which occurs if the file does not exist or the path is incorrect.
   - The second `catch` block handles general `IOException`, which could occur during reading operations (e.g., file corruption or access issues).

4. **Finally Block**: The `finally` block ensures that the `BufferedReader` is properly closed, even if an exception occurs during file reading.

Example Output:

If the `example.txt` file exists and is readable, the program will output the contents of the file:

```kotlin
```

```
Hello, this is a test file.
Welcome to Java Exception Handling.
```

If the file doesn't exist, the output will be:

```
javascript
```

```
Error: The file was not found.
```

Conclusion

In this chapter, you learned about **exception handling** in Java, which is essential for managing errors and ensuring the smooth execution of your programs. You explored how to use `try`, `catch`, and `finally` blocks to handle exceptions effectively. You also saw how to provide custom error messages, making your programs more user-friendly and resilient to errors.

Through the practical example of handling file reading exceptions, you gained a deeper understanding of how to deal with common file I/O errors and ensure that resources are properly managed. Exception handling not only helps in debugging but also ensures that the program can continue running or exit gracefully when errors occur.

As you continue to explore Java, mastering exception handling will be crucial for building robust applications that are easy to maintain and scale.

CHAPTER 13

COLLECTIONS FRAMEWORK IN JAVA

Understanding Collections: Lists, Sets, and Maps

The **Collections Framework** in Java provides a set of interfaces and classes to store and manipulate data in a structured way. Collections are objects that store multiple elements, and they provide various methods to perform operations like insertion, deletion, searching, and sorting. There are three core types of collections in Java:

1. **List**:
   - A `List` is an ordered collection that allows duplicates. Elements in a `List` are indexed, meaning you can access them using their position (index).
   - Lists maintain the order of elements as they were inserted.
   - **Common Implementations**: `ArrayList`, `LinkedList`.
2. **Set**:

o A `Set` is an unordered collection that does not allow duplicates. Each element can only appear once in a set, and there is no guarantee of the order in which elements are stored.

o **Common Implementations**: `HashSet`, `LinkedHashSet`, `TreeSet`.

3. **Map**:

o A `Map` is a collection that stores key-value pairs. Each key is unique, and it maps to exactly one value. Maps are useful for associating one object (the key) with another (the value).

o **Common Implementations**: `HashMap`, `LinkedHashMap`, `TreeMap`.

1. List

A `List` allows duplicate elements and maintains the order of insertion. Common `List` implementations include:

- **ArrayList**: Resizable array that allows fast random access to elements but slower insertions or deletions.
- **LinkedList**: Doubly-linked list that provides better performance for insertions or deletions at the beginning or middle, but slower random access.

Example of List:

```java

import java.util.ArrayList;
import java.util.List;

public class ListExample {
    public static void main(String[] args) {
        List<String> names = new ArrayList<>();
        names.add("Alice");
        names.add("Bob");
        names.add("Charlie");

        System.out.println("Names: " + names);
        System.out.println("Element at index 1:
" + names.get(1));  // Accessing element by index
    }
}
```

2. Set

A `Set` is used when you want to store unique elements and don't care about the order of those elements. Sets automatically eliminate duplicates. Common `Set` implementations include:

- **HashSet**: The most commonly used `Set` implementation, providing constant time performance for `add`, `remove`, and `contains` operations. It does not guarantee any specific order.

- **TreeSet**: A Set that maintains the elements in sorted order (natural ordering or according to a comparator).
- **LinkedHashSet**: A Set that maintains the insertion order of elements.

Example of Set:

java

```java
import java.util.HashSet;
import java.util.Set;

public class SetExample {
    public static void main(String[] args) {
        Set<String>    uniqueNames    =    new
HashSet<>();
        uniqueNames.add("Alice");
        uniqueNames.add("Bob");
        uniqueNames.add("Alice");   // Duplicate
entry, will be ignored

        System.out.println("Unique   names:   "  +
uniqueNames);
    }
}
```

3. Map

A Map stores key-value pairs, where each key is unique. A map is ideal for situations where you need to associate a value with a unique key. Common Map implementations include:

- **HashMap**: Provides constant time performance for basic operations (get, put, remove) but does not maintain any order.
- **LinkedHashMap**: Maintains the order of insertion of the key-value pairs.
- **TreeMap**: Maintains the keys in a sorted order.

Example of Map:

java

```
import java.util.HashMap;
import java.util.Map;

public class MapExample {
    public static void main(String[] args) {
        Map<String, Integer> phonebook = new HashMap<>();
        phonebook.put("Alice", 12345);
        phonebook.put("Bob", 67890);

        System.out.println("Phone number of Alice: " + phonebook.get("Alice"));
```

```
        System.out.println("Phonebook:      "      +
phonebook);
    }
}
```

When to Use Which Collection: Understanding the Use Cases of Different Collection Types

The choice of collection depends on your specific use case and the operations you need to perform.

1. **List**:
   o **Use when**: You need an ordered collection where duplicate elements are allowed, and you want to access elements by their index.
   o **Example Use Case**: Storing a list of items like names, tasks, or any other data where order matters.
   o **Best Implementations**: `ArrayList` for fast access, `LinkedList` for frequent insertions/deletions.
2. **Set**:
   o **Use when**: You need to store unique elements and do not care about the order.
   o **Example Use Case**: Storing unique items, such as a list of email addresses or tags, where duplicates are not allowed.

157

o **Best Implementations**: `HashSet` for fast access, `TreeSet` for ordered elements.

3. **Map**:

  o **Use when**: You need to store key-value pairs and require fast lookups using the key.

  o **Example Use Case**: Storing a dictionary (words as keys and definitions as values), or a user profile with a unique user ID as the key.

  o **Best Implementations**: `HashMap` for fast access, `TreeMap` for sorted keys, `LinkedHashMap` for maintaining insertion order.

Practical Example: Developing a Contact List Application Using a HashMap

Let's create a simple contact list application using a `HashMap`. In this application, we will store contact names as keys and their phone numbers as values.

Step 1: Define the Contact List Application

java

```
import java.util.HashMap;
import java.util.Map;
import java.util.Scanner;
```

```java
public class ContactList {
    public static void main(String[] args) {
        // Creating a HashMap to store contact names and their phone numbers
        Map<String, String> contacts = new HashMap<>();

        // Adding some initial contacts
        contacts.put("Alice", "123-456-7890");
        contacts.put("Bob", "987-654-3210");
        contacts.put("Charlie", "555-123-4567");

        // Scanner for user input
        Scanner scanner = new Scanner(System.in);

        // Display the menu
        System.out.println("Welcome to the Contact List Application!");
        System.out.println("1. View Contacts");
        System.out.println("2. Add a Contact");
        System.out.println("3. Search for a Contact");
        System.out.println("4. Exit");

        // Simple menu loop
        int choice;
        do {
```

```java
            System.out.print("Enter your choice: ");
            choice = scanner.nextInt();
            scanner.nextLine();   // Consume the newline

            switch (choice) {
                case 1:
                    // Display all contacts
System.out.println("Contacts:");
                    for     (Map.Entry<String, String> entry : contacts.entrySet()) {

System.out.println(entry.getKey()   +   ":   "   +   entry.getValue());
                    }
                    break;

                case 2:
                    // Add a new contact
                    System.out.print("Enter name: ");
                    String     name     = scanner.nextLine();
                    System.out.print("Enter phone number: ");
                    String     phoneNumber     = scanner.nextLine();
```

160

```
                    contacts.put(name,
phoneNumber);
                    System.out.println("Contact
added successfully!");
                    break;

            case 3:
                // Search for a contact
                System.out.print("Enter name
to search: ");
                String      searchName      =
scanner.nextLine();
                if
(contacts.containsKey(searchName)) {

System.out.println(searchName    ":    "    +
contacts.get(searchName));
                } else {

System.out.println("Contact not found!");
                }
                break;

            case 4:
                System.out.println("Exiting
the application.");
                break;

            default:
```

```
                System.out.println("Invalid
choice, please try again.");
        }
    } while (choice != 4);

        scanner.close();
    }
}
```

Explanation of the Code:

1. **Contact Storage**:
   - We use a HashMap to store contacts, where the contact name is the key (e.g., "Alice") and the phone number is the value (e.g., "123-456-7890").

2. **Menu and User Interaction**:
   - A simple menu allows the user to view all contacts, add a new contact, or search for a contact.

3. **Adding a Contact**:
   - The user can input a contact name and phone number, and this information is stored in the HashMap using the put() method.

4. **Searching for a Contact**:
   - The program allows users to search for a contact by name using containsKey() to check if the

162

contact exists and `get()` to retrieve the phone number.

Example Output:

vbnet

Welcome to the Contact List Application!
1. View Contacts
2. Add a Contact
3. Search for a Contact
4. Exit
Enter your choice: 1
Contacts:
Alice: 123-456-7890
Bob: 987-654-3210
Charlie: 555-123-4567

Conclusion

In this chapter, we explored the Java **Collections Framework**, focusing on the most commonly used collection types: **Lists**, **Sets**, and **Maps**. We discussed their characteristics, differences, and when to use each type, helping you choose the right collection for different scenarios.

Through the practical example of a contact list application using a `HashMap`, you saw how easy it is to store key-value pairs and manipulate them with various methods like `put()`, `get()`, and `containsKey()`.

Mastering the collections framework is crucial for working with large datasets, as it provides efficient ways to store, access, and manipulate data. In the next chapters, we will continue building on your Java skills with more advanced topics like sorting collections and handling concurrency.

CHAPTER 14

JAVA GENERICS – MAKING CODE FLEXIBLE

What are Generics? Understanding How to Write Type-Safe Code

Java Generics is a feature introduced in Java 5 that allows you to write **type-safe** code. By using generics, you can define classes, interfaces, and methods with type parameters, ensuring that they can operate on objects of any type while maintaining strong type checks at compile time. This adds flexibility to your code and reduces runtime errors by catching type mismatches during the compilation process.

1. What Do Generics Do?

Generics allow you to create classes, methods, and interfaces that can work with any type of object, while still maintaining type safety. This means that you can write code that is independent of data types, but without losing the benefits of the strong typing system that Java provides.

Without Generics: When you don't use generics, you might have to cast objects to specific types, which can result in `ClassCastException` at runtime if the wrong type is cast.

With Generics: You specify a type parameter, and the compiler ensures that the objects used with that class, method, or interface match the specified type. This eliminates the need for casting and provides compile-time type checking.

2. Syntax of Generics

To use generics in Java, you use angle brackets (<>) to specify a type parameter. This can be done in the following scenarios:

- **Generic Class**: A class that works with a type parameter.
- **Generic Method**: A method that works with a type parameter.
- **Generic Interface**: An interface that works with a type parameter.

The type parameter is often represented by a single uppercase letter, such as T (for Type), E (for Element), K (for Key), V (for Value), and so on.

Example:

```java
java
```

166

```
class Box<T> {
    private T value;

    public void setValue(T value) {
        this.value = value;
    }

    public T getValue() {
        return value;
    }
}
```

In this example, T is a placeholder for the type that will be specified when you create an instance of the Box class.

3. Benefits of Using Generics

1. **Type Safety**: Generics allow the compiler to check that you are using the correct type when interacting with objects.

2. **Elimination of Casting**: Without generics, you often need to cast objects to the appropriate type. With generics, this is not necessary.

3. **Code Reusability**: You can write more flexible and reusable code that can work with any data type.

Practical Example: Creating a Box Class That Can Store Objects of Any Type

Let's build a simple `Box` class using generics, which can store objects of any type. The class will have methods to set and get the value stored inside the box.

Step 1: Define the Generic Box Class

java

```java
// Define a generic class Box
class Box<T> {
    private T value;   // Declare a variable of type T

    // Method to set the value of the box
    public void setValue(T value) {
        this.value = value;
    }

    // Method to get the value from the box
    public T getValue() {
        return value;
    }
}
```

In this example:

- T represents the type of the object that will be stored in the box. This could be any type: Integer, String, or any custom class type.
- The setValue() method allows us to set the value, while getValue() allows us to retrieve it.

Step 2: Use the Box Class with Different Data Types

Now that we have a Box class that works with any type, we can create instances of Box with different types and demonstrate how the generic Box class works.

java

```
public class TestBox {
    public static void main(String[] args) {
        // Create a Box for storing an Integer
        Box<Integer> intBox = new Box<>();
        intBox.setValue(100);     // Store an
Integer value in the Box
        System.out.println("Integer Value: " +
intBox.getValue());  // Retrieve and print the
Integer value

        // Create a Box for storing a String
        Box<String> strBox = new Box<>();
        strBox.setValue("Hello, Generics!");  //
Store a String value in the Box
```

```
        System.out.println("String Value: " +
strBox.getValue());  // Retrieve and print the
String value

        // Create a Box for storing a custom type
(e.g., a Date object)
        Box<java.util.Date> dateBox = new
Box<>();
        dateBox.setValue(new java.util.Date());
// Store a Date object in the Box
        System.out.println("Date Value: " +
dateBox.getValue());  // Retrieve and print the
Date object
    }
}
```

Explanation of the Code:

1. **Creating Box Objects**:
   o We created three `Box` objects: `intBox`, `strBox`, and `dateBox`, each using a different data type (`Integer`, `String`, and `Date`, respectively).

2. **Using the `setValue()` and `getValue()` Methods**:
   o For each box, we set a value using the `setValue()` method and retrieved it using the `getValue()` method.

3. **Generics in Action**:
   o The type of each `Box` (whether `Integer`, `String`, or `Date`) is specified when creating the

170

object, ensuring that the correct type is used, and preventing type-related errors.

Example Output:

```yaml
yaml

Integer Value: 100
String Value: Hello, Generics!
Date Value: Tue Apr 06 12:59:01 GMT 2022
```

In this example:

- The `Box` class worked seamlessly with different data types. The compiler ensures that each box only stores the correct type of object, so there is no need for casting, and type safety is guaranteed.

Additional Features of Generics

1. **Bounded Type Parameters**: Sometimes, you might want to restrict the types that can be used with a generic class or method. You can achieve this by using bounded type parameters.

   Example:

   ```java
   java
   ```

```
class Box<T extends Number> {  // T must be
a subclass of Number
    private T value;
    public void setValue(T value) {
        this.value = value;
    }
    public T getValue() {
        return value;
    }
}
```

In this case, the generic type T is bounded by Number, so the Box can only accept objects that are subclasses of Number (e.g., Integer, Double, Float).

2. **Wildcards**: The wildcard (?) allows you to specify that a method can accept any type. For example, Box<?> can accept a Box of any type, but it restricts you from modifying the value inside the box.

Example:

```
java
```

```
public void printBoxValue(Box<?> box) {
    System.out.println("Value:       "    +
box.getValue());
}
```

The wildcard ? represents an unknown type, making it more flexible when you don't need to know the exact type at compile time.

Conclusion

In this chapter, we explored **Java Generics**, which allow you to write flexible, reusable, and type-safe code. By using generics, you can create classes, interfaces, and methods that work with different types while maintaining type safety at compile time. We demonstrated how to implement a `Box` class that can store objects of any type, and you saw how generics eliminate the need for casting and prevent type errors.

Generics improve the flexibility and maintainability of your code, making it easier to work with collections, data structures, and algorithms. As you continue your Java journey, mastering generics will be crucial for building robust, scalable, and type-safe applications.

In the next chapters, we'll dive into more advanced topics like sorting and working with collections in more depth.

CHAPTER 15

JAVA STREAMS AND LAMBDA EXPRESSIONS

Introduction to Streams: Working with Collections Using Functional-Style Operations

Introduced in Java 8, **Streams** provide a functional approach to working with collections (like `List`, `Set`, `Map`, etc.). A stream represents a sequence of elements that can be processed in parallel or sequentially. It enables functional-style operations like filtering, mapping, reducing, and more.

Streams provide a high-level abstraction for processing collections of data, allowing you to write concise, readable, and efficient code. They are particularly useful when you need to perform operations on large datasets, and they support both **sequential** and **parallel** processing.

1. Key Concepts of Streams

- **Stream Operations**: Streams provide a set of methods for performing operations like filtering, mapping, and reducing. Operations can be classified into two categories:

1. **Intermediate operations**: These operations return a new stream and are **lazy**, meaning they do not execute until a terminal operation is invoked (e.g., `filter()`, `map()`, `sorted()`).

2. **Terminal operations**: These operations produce a result or a side effect and mark the end of the stream pipeline (e.g., `collect()`, `forEach()`, `reduce()`).

- **Chaining**: Streams support **method chaining**, where you can combine multiple operations in a fluent way.

- **Parallel Streams**: Streams can be processed in parallel, utilizing multiple cores of the CPU for performance improvement on large datasets.

2. Basic Syntax of Streams

To create a stream from a collection, you can use the `stream()` method. Once you have a stream, you can apply various operations on it.

Example:

```java

import java.util.Arrays;
import java.util.List;
```

```java
import java.util.stream.Collectors;

public class StreamExample {
    public static void main(String[] args) {
        List<String>            names            =
Arrays.asList("Alice",      "Bob",      "Charlie",
"David", "Eve");

        // Using Stream to filter names starting
with "A"
        List<String>            filteredNames            =
names.stream()

.filter(name -> name.startsWith("A"))

.collect(Collectors.toList());

        System.out.println(filteredNames);     //
Output: [Alice]
    }
}
```

In this example:

- names.stream() creates a stream from the List.
- filter(name -> name.startsWith("A")) is an intermediate operation that filters the stream based on the condition.

- `collect(Collectors.toList())` is a terminal operation that collects the filtered stream into a new list.

3. Common Stream Operations

- **filter()**: Filters elements based on a condition.
- **map()**: Transforms elements into another form.
- **forEach()**: Iterates over elements.
- **reduce()**: Reduces the stream to a single value.
- **collect()**: Collects the result of a stream into a collection (e.g., `List`, `Set`).

Lambda Expressions: Writing Concise, Readable Code Using Lambda Functions

Lambda expressions, also introduced in Java 8, enable you to write more concise and readable code by allowing you to pass behavior (methods) as parameters to functions. A lambda expression represents an anonymous function (a function with no name) that can be used to implement methods defined by functional interfaces.

1. Syntax of Lambda Expressions

Lambda expressions consist of three parts:

- **Parameters**: The input values to the function.
- **Arrow (->)**: Separates parameters from the body.
- **Body**: The logic of the function.

Basic Syntax:

```java

(parameters) -> expression
```

Example:

```java

// Lambda expression for adding two numbers
(int a, int b) -> a + b
```

2. Lambda Expression in Action

You can use lambda expressions to implement functional interfaces like `Runnable`, `Comparator`, or even custom interfaces. One of the most common uses of lambdas is in conjunction with Streams.

Example:

```java

import java.util.Arrays;
import java.util.List;
```

178

```
public class LambdaExample {
    public static void main(String[] args) {
        List<String>          names          =
Arrays.asList("Alice",      "Bob",       "Charlie",
"David", "Eve");

        // Using lambda expression with forEach
to print each name
        names.forEach(name                    ->
System.out.println(name));
    }
}
```

In this example:

- `names.forEach(name` `->` `System.out.println(name))` uses a lambda expression to print each element of the list.
- The lambda expression `name` `->` `System.out.println(name)` specifies what should happen for each element in the list.

3. Benefits of Lambda Expressions

- **Concise Code**: Lambda expressions allow you to write more compact code by removing boilerplate code such as anonymous inner classes.

179

- **Improved Readability**: The code is more readable and expressive, especially when using it in functional-style operations like Streams.

Practical Example: Filtering and Transforming a List of Employees Using Java Streams

Let's put these concepts into practice by building an example of processing a list of `Employee` objects using Java Streams and Lambda expressions.

Step 1: Define the Employee Class
java

```java
class Employee {
    String name;
    int age;
    double salary;

    public Employee(String name, int age, double salary) {
        this.name = name;
        this.age = age;
        this.salary = salary;
    }

    public String getName() {
```

```
        return name;
    }

    public int getAge() {
        return age;
    }

    public double getSalary() {
        return salary;
    }

    @Override
    public String toString() {
        return "Employee{name='" + name + "',
age=" + age + ", salary=" + salary + "}";
    }
}
```

Step 2: Create and Process the List of Employees

Now, let's create a list of `Employee` objects and use Streams and Lambda expressions to filter and transform the data. For example, we will:

1. Filter employees who are older than 30.
2. Increase their salary by 10%.
3. Collect and print the transformed list.

```
java
```

181

```java
import java.util.Arrays;
import java.util.List;
import java.util.stream.Collectors;

public class EmployeeStreamExample {
    public static void main(String[] args) {
        List<Employee> employees = Arrays.asList(
                new Employee("Alice", 28, 50000),
                new Employee("Bob", 35, 60000),
                new Employee("Charlie", 40, 70000),
                new Employee("David", 30, 80000),
                new Employee("Eve", 45, 90000)
        );

        // Filter employees older than 30 and increase their salary by 10%
        List<Employee> updatedEmployees = employees.stream()
                .filter(e -> e.getAge() > 30) // Filter employees older than 30
                .map(e -> new Employee(e.getName(), e.getAge(), e.getSalary() * 1.1)) // Increase salary by 10%
                .collect(Collectors.toList()); // Collect into a new list
```

```
    // Print the updated list

updatedEmployees.forEach(System.out::println);
    }
}
```

Explanation of the Code:

1. `filter(e -> e.getAge() > 30)`: This filters the employees, keeping only those who are older than 30.

2. `map(e -> new Employee(e.getName(), e.getAge(), e.getSalary() * 1.1))`: This transforms each employee by increasing their salary by 10%.

3. `collect(Collectors.toList())`: This collects the results into a new list.

4. `forEach(System.out::println)`: This prints each employee in the updated list.

Example Output:

pgsql

```
Employee{name='Bob', age=35, salary=66000.0}
Employee{name='Charlie', age=40, salary=77000.0}
Employee{name='David', age=30, salary=88000.0}
Employee{name='Eve', age=45, salary=99000.0}
```

In this example:

- We first filtered employees based on their age and then used map () to transform their salaries by increasing them by 10%.

- The final list contains only employees older than 30, with their salaries updated.

Conclusion

In this chapter, we explored **Java Streams** and **Lambda Expressions**, two powerful features introduced in Java 8 that enable you to write more concise, functional-style code. Streams provide a declarative way to process collections, while lambda expressions simplify code by allowing you to pass behavior as parameters.

Through the practical example of filtering and transforming a list of employees, you saw how easy it is to manipulate data using streams and lambdas. These tools are invaluable for writing clean, efficient, and maintainable code, especially when working with large datasets.

In the next chapters, we will delve deeper into more advanced topics like **parallel streams**, **custom collectors**, and **exception handling** to further enhance your Java programming skills.

Part 5

Concurrency and Performance in Java

CHAPTER 16

THREADS AND

MULTITHREADING IN JAVA

What are Threads? Understanding How Multithreading Works in Java

A **thread** is the smallest unit of execution within a program. In a multithreaded application, multiple threads can run concurrently, enabling your program to perform several tasks at the same time. This is particularly useful in modern computers with multi-core processors, where each thread can potentially run on a different core, improving performance and responsiveness.

Java provides robust support for multithreading, which allows you to write programs that can perform multiple tasks simultaneously. Multithreading can be particularly useful in scenarios like handling user input, performing background tasks, or processing large datasets.

1. Key Concepts of Threads

- **Thread Lifecycle**: A thread goes through several states during its lifetime:

- o **New**: A thread is created but not yet started.

- o **Runnable**: The thread is ready to run and waiting for CPU time.

- o **Blocked**: The thread is waiting for a resource (like I/O) to become available.

- o **Terminated**: The thread has completed its task and terminated.

- **Thread Scheduling**: The operating system's thread scheduler controls which thread runs at any given time. The JVM (Java Virtual Machine) manages thread scheduling on top of the OS's scheduling mechanism.

- **Concurrency vs Parallelism**:
  - o **Concurrency**: Multiple threads can make progress at the same time, but they may not necessarily be executed simultaneously.
  - o **Parallelism**: Multiple threads are executed simultaneously on multi-core processors.

2. Why Use Threads?

- **Responsiveness**: Multithreading helps keep the application responsive. For example, in a GUI application, one thread might be handling user input while another is processing data in the background.

- **Better Resource Utilization**: By using multiple threads, you can take advantage of multi-core processors, allowing your program to run more efficiently.

Creating and Managing Threads: Using the Thread Class and Runnable Interface

In Java, you can create and manage threads in two main ways:

1. **Extending the Thread class**
2. **Implementing the Runnable interface**

Let's go through each method.

1. Creating a Thread by Extending the Thread Class

To create a thread by extending the `Thread` class, you need to:

- Create a new class that extends `Thread`.
- Override the `run()` method to define the code that should run in the new thread.
- Create an instance of your class and call `start()` to begin the thread's execution.

Example:

```java

class MyThread extends Thread {
    @Override
    public void run() {
```

```
        // Code to be executed in the new thread
        System.out.println("Thread            is
running.");
    }
}


public class ThreadExample {
    public static void main(String[] args) {
        MyThread thread = new MyThread();    //
Create a new thread
        thread.start();  // Start the thread
    }
}
```

In this example:

- MyThread extends the Thread class and overrides the run() method, which contains the code to be executed by the thread.
- We create an instance of MyThread and start it with thread.start().

2. Creating a Thread by Implementing the Runnable Interface

An alternative to extending the Thread class is to implement the Runnable interface. This allows you to implement the run() method without needing to extend Thread. This method is often preferred, especially when you need to extend another class that is not Thread.

Steps to create a thread using Runnable:

- Implement the Runnable interface.
- Define the run() method with the code you want to execute.
- Pass an instance of the Runnable implementation to a Thread object and start the thread.

Example:

```java

class MyRunnable implements Runnable {
    @Override
    public void run() {
        // Code to be executed in the new thread
        System.out.println("Runnable thread is
running.");
    }
}

public class RunnableExample {
    public static void main(String[] args) {
        MyRunnable runnable = new MyRunnable();
// Create a Runnable object
```

```
        Thread thread = new Thread(runnable);
// Pass it to a Thread object
        thread.start();  // Start the thread
    }
}
```

In this example:

- `MyRunnable` implements `Runnable` and provides the `run()` method that defines the task to be performed in the thread.
- We create a `Thread` object by passing `MyRunnable` to it, and then start the thread with `thread.start()`.

Practical Example: A Simple Program That Simulates a Multi-threaded ATM

Let's build a simple multi-threaded ATM simulation where multiple customers can use the ATM simultaneously. Each customer will perform different tasks, such as checking the balance, withdrawing money, and depositing money.

In this example, we will simulate each task in a separate thread to demonstrate how multithreading works in Java.

Step 1: Define the ATM Class (Shared Resource)

We will create an ATM class that represents the ATM machine, with methods to check balance, withdraw, and deposit.

java

```
class ATM {
    private double balance;

    public ATM(double balance) {
        this.balance = balance;
    }

    // Synchronized methods to ensure thread-safety
    public synchronized void checkBalance() {
        System.out.println("Checking balance: "
+ balance);
    }

    public synchronized void withdraw(double
amount) {
        if (amount <= balance) {
            balance -= amount;
            System.out.println("Withdrew:    "    +
amount + ". Remaining balance: " + balance);
        } else {
```

```
        System.out.println("Insufficient
funds.");
        }
    }


    public   synchronized   void   deposit(double
amount) {
        balance += amount;
        System.out.println("Deposited:     "     +
amount + ". New balance: " + balance);
    }
}
```

- The ATM class has a balance field representing the ATM balance.
- The checkBalance(), withdraw(), and deposit() methods are **synchronized** to prevent multiple threads from modifying the balance simultaneously and causing inconsistent results.

Step 2: Define the Customer Thread

Each customer will perform operations on the ATM, and we will simulate each customer's actions in a separate thread.

java

```
class Customer implements Runnable {
    private ATM atm;
```

```
private String name;

public Customer(ATM atm, String name) {
    this.atm = atm;
    this.name = name;
}

@Override
public void run() {
    atm.checkBalance();
    atm.withdraw(100);
    atm.deposit(200);
}
}
```

- The `Customer` class implements `Runnable` and simulates a customer interacting with the ATM. Each customer checks their balance, withdraws money, and deposits money.
- These actions will be executed in separate threads.

Step 3: Run the Program with Multiple Customers

In the `main()` method, we will create an `ATM` object and multiple `Customer` objects, each representing a different thread.

java

```
public class ATMSimulation {
```

194

```
public static void main(String[] args) {
    ATM atm = new ATM(1000);  // Create an
ATM with an initial balance of 1000

    // Create customer threads
    Thread customer1 = new Thread(new
Customer(atm, "Customer 1"));
    Thread customer2 = new Thread(new
Customer(atm, "Customer 2"));
    Thread customer3 = new Thread(new
Customer(atm, "Customer 3"));

    // Start the customer threads
    customer1.start();
    customer2.start();
    customer3.start();
    }
}
```

- The ATM object is shared between all customer threads.
- Each customer runs in their own thread and performs actions on the ATM.
- The actions are synchronized to ensure that the balance is updated correctly.

Example Output:

yaml

Checking balance: 1000.0

195

```
Withdrew: 100.0. Remaining balance: 900.0
Deposited: 200.0. New balance: 1100.0
Checking balance: 1100.0
Withdrew: 100.0. Remaining balance: 1000.0
Deposited: 200.0. New balance: 1200.0
Checking balance: 1200.0
Withdrew: 100.0. Remaining balance: 1100.0
Deposited: 200.0. New balance: 1300.0
```

In this example, the ATM is accessed by multiple customers simultaneously, each performing operations like checking the balance, withdrawing money, and depositing money. The synchronized methods ensure thread-safety and prevent inconsistent balance updates.

Conclusion

In this chapter, you learned about **threads** and **multithreading** in Java, and how multithreading can help you write more efficient and responsive applications. You saw how to create and manage threads using both the `Thread` class and the `Runnable` interface. Additionally, you learned about **synchronization**, which is essential for ensuring that multiple threads can safely interact with shared resources, such as in our ATM simulation.

By understanding multithreading, you can take full advantage of modern hardware with multiple cores and build applications that perform efficiently even under heavy load. In the next chapters, we will dive into more advanced concurrency topics such as **Executor Services**, **Thread Pools**, and **Performance Optimization**.

CHAPTER 17

SYNCHRONIZATION IN JAVA

The Importance of Synchronization: Handling Shared Resources in Multithreaded Programs

In a multithreaded environment, multiple threads can simultaneously access and modify shared resources. This can lead to **race conditions**, where the outcome of operations depends on the timing of thread execution, potentially causing inconsistent or incorrect results. **Synchronization** is a mechanism in Java that ensures that only one thread can access a resource at a time, preventing race conditions and ensuring thread safety.

1. What is Synchronization?

Synchronization in Java is used to control access to shared resources in a multithreaded environment. When multiple threads access the same resource, synchronization ensures that only one thread at a time can access that resource, which prevents **data inconsistency** and **corruption**.

- **Synchronized Methods**: A method can be marked as `synchronized`, meaning that only one thread can execute that method at a time for an object. This prevents other threads from accessing the method until the current thread finishes execution.

- **Synchronized Blocks**: In addition to synchronizing entire methods, you can also synchronize specific blocks of code within a method. This provides more granular control over the synchronization process.

2. Why Synchronization is Important?

When multiple threads are working with shared resources (like variables or objects), the changes made by one thread might not be visible to other threads, or the operations might interfere with each other. This can lead to inconsistent results. Synchronization helps to:

- Prevent multiple threads from simultaneously modifying the same data.
- Ensure that the resources are accessed in a controlled manner, avoiding conflicts and corruption.

Example of a Race Condition: Consider a scenario where two threads are trying to update the same bank account balance at the same time. If there is no synchronization, one thread might overwrite the updates made by the other thread, resulting in an incorrect final balance.

Practical Example: Preventing Race Conditions in a Bank Account Application

In this example, we will simulate a **bank account** class where multiple threads can attempt to withdraw money from the account at the same time. Without synchronization, a race condition could occur, causing the balance to be incorrect after multiple withdrawals. We will use synchronization to prevent this issue.

Step 1: Define the Bank Account Class

We will create a `BankAccount` class that allows money to be deposited and withdrawn. Without synchronization, multiple threads could interfere with each other when modifying the account balance.

java

```java
class BankAccount {
    private double balance;

    // Constructor to initialize the balance
    public BankAccount(double balance) {
        this.balance = balance;
    }

    // Method to withdraw money without
synchronization (may cause race condition)
    public void withdraw(double amount) {
```

```
        if (balance >= amount) {

System.out.println(Thread.currentThread().getNa
me() + " is withdrawing: " + amount);
            balance -= amount;
            System.out.println("New balance: " +
balance);
        } else {
            System.out.println("Insufficient
funds for " + Thread.currentThread().getName());
        }
    }

    // Method to check the balance
    public double getBalance() {
        return balance;
    }
}
```

In this example, the withdraw() method allows a thread to withdraw money from the account. If two threads try to withdraw money at the same time, they may both read the same balance before either thread updates it, leading to an incorrect final balance.

Step 2: Introduce Synchronization to Prevent Race Conditions

We will now modify the `withdraw()` method to make it **synchronized**. This will prevent more than one thread from accessing the method at the same time.

```java
class BankAccount {
    private double balance;

    // Constructor to initialize the balance
    public BankAccount(double balance) {
        this.balance = balance;
    }

    // Synchronized method to withdraw money
    public synchronized void withdraw(double amount) {
        if (balance >= amount) {

System.out.println(Thread.currentThread().getName() + " is withdrawing: " + amount);
            balance -= amount;
            System.out.println("New balance: " + balance);
        } else {
            System.out.println("Insufficient funds for " + Thread.currentThread().getName());
```

```
        }
    }

    // Method to check the balance
    public double getBalance() {
        return balance;
    }
}
```

Now, the `withdraw()` method is synchronized, which means that only one thread can execute it at a time. If a thread is executing the `withdraw()` method, other threads will be blocked until the first thread completes the operation, thus preventing race conditions.

Step 3: Simulate Multiple Threads Accessing the Bank Account

Let's now simulate multiple threads (representing different customers) trying to withdraw money from the same bank account at the same time.

java

```
class Customer extends Thread {
    private BankAccount account;
    private double amount;

    public Customer(BankAccount account, double
amount) {
```

```java
            this.account = account;
            this.amount = amount;
    }

    @Override
    public void run() {
        account.withdraw(amount);
    }
}

public class BankSimulation {
    public static void main(String[] args) {
        BankAccount         account        =        new
BankAccount(500);   // Initial balance: 500

        // Creating  multiple  customer  threads
(simulating customers withdrawing money)
        Customer        customer1        =        new
Customer(account, 200);
        Customer        customer2        =        new
Customer(account, 300);
        Customer        customer3        =        new
Customer(account, 100);

        // Starting  the  threads  (simulating
concurrent access)
        customer1.start();
        customer2.start();
        customer3.start();
```

```
    }
}
```

Explanation of the Code:

1. **Customer Class**: The `Customer` class extends `Thread` and simulates a customer attempting to withdraw money from the bank account. Each customer is assigned an amount to withdraw when the thread is created.

2. **BankSimulation Class**: In the `main()` method, we create a `BankAccount` object with an initial balance of 500. Then, we create three customer threads, each attempting to withdraw a different amount. The threads are started concurrently, simulating multiple customers accessing the bank account at the same time.

3. **Synchronization**: The `withdraw()` method is synchronized to ensure that only one customer can withdraw money at a time, preventing race conditions and ensuring the correct final balance.

Example Output:

vbnet

```
Thread-0 is withdrawing: 200.0
New balance: 300.0
Thread-1 is withdrawing: 300.0
New balance: 0.0
Thread-2 is withdrawing: 100.0
Insufficient funds for Thread-2
```

In this output:

- `Thread-0` successfully withdraws 200.
- `Thread-1` successfully withdraws 300, leaving the balance at 0.
- `Thread-2` tries to withdraw 100 but encounters an "insufficient funds" message because the balance is now 0.

Without Synchronization (Example of a Race Condition)

If we remove the `synchronized` keyword from the `withdraw()` method, the program may exhibit inconsistent results due to race conditions. Two or more threads could read the balance before it's updated, resulting in incorrect withdrawals. For example, both threads could think there is enough money in the account and try to withdraw money, even if there isn't enough.

Conclusion

In this chapter, you learned about **synchronization** in Java and how it helps in managing shared resources in a multithreaded environment. By using the `synchronized` keyword, we ensured that only one thread could access the critical section of the code (the `withdraw()` method) at a time, preventing race conditions and ensuring thread safety.

206

Through the practical example of a bank account application, you saw how multiple threads can safely interact with shared resources using synchronization. This knowledge is crucial for building thread-safe applications that handle concurrent tasks reliably.

In the next chapters, we will explore more advanced concurrency topics such as **Executor Services**, **Thread Pools**, and **Concurrency Utilities** to improve performance and scalability in Java applications.

CHAPTER 18

OPTIMIZING PERFORMANCE IN JAVA

Performance Bottlenecks: Identifying and Resolving Performance Issues

In any application, performance bottlenecks can lead to slower execution, higher resource consumption, and overall inefficiency. Identifying and addressing performance bottlenecks is crucial to ensuring that your application runs smoothly, especially when dealing with large-scale systems, high traffic, or resource-intensive tasks.

1. Common Performance Bottlenecks in Java Applications

- **CPU Usage**: High CPU usage could be caused by inefficient algorithms, unnecessary computations, or excessive thread context switching.
- **Memory Leaks**: Memory leaks occur when objects are no longer needed but are not properly garbage collected. This can lead to excessive memory usage and eventually cause `OutOfMemoryError`.

- **I/O Operations**: Input/Output (I/O) operations, such as reading from disk or network, can often become a bottleneck, especially when handled synchronously or inefficiently.

- **Database Queries**: Poorly optimized database queries, lack of indexing, or excessive database connections can slow down data retrieval and updates.

- **Thread Management**: Excessive or poorly managed threads can lead to high context-switching overhead and wasted CPU cycles. Proper thread pooling and management are essential.

2. Identifying Performance Bottlenecks

To identify performance bottlenecks, you can use a variety of tools and techniques:

- **Profiling**: Profiling tools like **JProfiler**, **VisualVM**, or **YourKit** help you track CPU usage, memory consumption, and thread activity. They provide detailed insights into where your program spends the most time and which resources it consumes.

- **Logging**: Inserting performance-related logging at critical points in the code (e.g., method entry/exit) can help identify areas where time is being spent.

- **Benchmarking**: Benchmarking libraries like **JMH (Java Microbenchmarking Harness)** can be used to measure the performance of specific methods or operations in your program.

3. Resolving Performance Issues

Once you've identified bottlenecks, the next step is to resolve them:

- **Optimize Algorithms**: Evaluate whether your algorithms are the most efficient ones. Switching from a brute-force approach to more efficient algorithms can significantly improve performance (e.g., using a binary search instead of a linear search).
- **Reduce I/O Operations**: Minimize disk and network I/O by using buffered streams, caching results, or reading large chunks of data at once.
- **Optimize Database Access**: Use prepared statements, batch updates, and indexing to speed up database operations. Avoid opening new connections frequently by using connection pooling.
- **Thread Pooling**: Instead of creating new threads for each task, use **ExecutorService** to manage a pool of worker threads that can execute tasks concurrently, reducing overhead and improving resource utilization.

Garbage Collection: How Java Manages Memory and What You Need to Know

Garbage collection (GC) in Java is an automatic process that reclaims memory by destroying objects that are no longer reachable or needed. This helps Java manage memory efficiently and prevents memory leaks without the programmer having to manually allocate and deallocate memory.

1. How Garbage Collection Works

The **Java Garbage Collector** (GC) identifies objects in memory that are no longer referenced by any part of the application and reclaims their memory for reuse. The main steps involved in garbage collection are:

1. **Marking**: The GC identifies which objects are still being referenced and marks them as reachable.
2. **Sweeping**: The GC then collects all objects that are no longer reachable (unreferenced) and reclaims their memory.
3. **Compacting**: The GC may also compact memory to reduce fragmentation, ensuring that free memory is contiguous.

211

2. Types of Garbage Collectors

Java provides several types of garbage collectors, each optimized for different use cases. The most common types are:

- **Serial GC**: A simple garbage collector that uses a single thread for garbage collection. Suitable for single-threaded applications or environments with limited resources.
- **Parallel GC**: Also known as throughput-oriented garbage collector, it uses multiple threads for garbage collection and is suitable for multi-threaded applications.
- **CMS (Concurrent Mark-Sweep) GC**: A low-latency garbage collector designed to minimize pause times. Suitable for applications where low latency is a critical factor.
- **G1 GC**: A garbage collector designed to handle large heaps with low pause times. It divides the heap into regions and performs garbage collection concurrently with the application.

3. Understanding Garbage Collection Tuning

Although garbage collection is automatic, it can be tuned for better performance, especially in applications with large memory usage. The most common tuning techniques are:

- **Heap Size**: Adjusting the heap size can have a significant impact on GC performance. Use -Xms to set the initial heap size and -Xmx to set the maximum heap size.

- **GC Pause Time**: You can control the pause time during garbage collection by using the -XX:MaxGCPauseMillis option, which sets the target maximum pause time.

- **Garbage Collector Selection**: Depending on your application's needs (throughput, latency, etc.), you can choose the most appropriate garbage collector. For example, use -XX:+UseG1GC for G1 GC.

4. Monitoring Garbage Collection

To monitor and understand the garbage collection behavior in your application, you can enable GC logging:

bash

```
java -Xlog:gc* -jar MyApplication.jar
```

This will provide logs showing the activity of the garbage collector, including the amount of memory reclaimed, the number of GC pauses, and their durations.

Practical Example: Performance Optimization of a Database Connection Pooling System

A **database connection pool** is a collection of reusable database connections. Using a connection pool improves performance by reducing the overhead of opening and closing database connections frequently.

In this practical example, we will demonstrate how to optimize the performance of a database connection pooling system.

Step 1: Simple Database Connection Pooling

A basic connection pool can be implemented using a `LinkedList` to store available connections. When a request for a connection comes in, a connection is retrieved from the pool. After the work is done, the connection is returned to the pool.

```java
import java.sql.Connection;
import java.sql.DriverManager;
import java.sql.SQLException;
import java.util.LinkedList;

public class ConnectionPool {
    private static final int MAX_CONNECTIONS =
10;
```

```java
    private            LinkedList<Connection>
availableConnections;
    private       String       dbUrl       =
"jdbc:mysql://localhost:3306/mydatabase";
    private String dbUser = "root";
    private String dbPassword = "password";

    public ConnectionPool() {
        availableConnections          =          new
LinkedList<>();
        try {
            // Initialize the pool with a certain
number of connections
            for (int i = 0; i < MAX_CONNECTIONS;
i++) {

availableConnections.add(DriverManager.getConne
ction(dbUrl, dbUser, dbPassword));
            }
        } catch (SQLException e) {
            e.printStackTrace();
        }
    }

    // Get a connection from the pool
    public       synchronized       Connection
getConnection() {
        if (availableConnections.isEmpty()) {
```

215

```
        System.out.println("No      available
connections.");
            return null;
        } else {
            return
availableConnections.removeFirst();
        }
    }


    // Return a connection to the pool
    public            synchronized            void
releaseConnection(Connection connection) {
        if (connection != null) {

availableConnections.addLast(connection);
        }
    }
}
```

Step 2: Performance Bottleneck: Synchronized Methods

In the above implementation, the getConnection() and releaseConnection() methods are synchronized. This can create a performance bottleneck if there are many threads trying to access the connection pool concurrently, as they are blocked until the lock is released.

Step 3: Optimizing the Connection Pool

To improve performance, we can use a more efficient threading model, such as using an **ExecutorService** for handling threads, or we can reduce synchronization overhead by allowing multiple threads to perform non-critical tasks concurrently.

A more advanced approach involves using **Apache Commons DBCP** or **HikariCP**, which are specialized libraries for managing database connection pools. These libraries are highly optimized for performance and provide features like automatic connection validation and pooling.

Step 4: Optimized Connection Pool Using HikariCP

java

```
import com.zaxxer.hikari.HikariConfig;
import com.zaxxer.hikari.HikariDataSource;

public class OptimizedConnectionPool {
    private static HikariDataSource dataSource;

    static {
        HikariConfig     config     =     new
HikariConfig();

config.setJdbcUrl("jdbc:mysql://localhost:3306/
mydatabase");
        config.setUsername("root");
```

217

```
        config.setPassword("password");
        config.setMaximumPoolSize(10);        //
Maximum number of connections in the pool


        dataSource              =              new
HikariDataSource(config);
    }


    // Get a connection from the pool
    public   static   Connection   getConnection()
throws SQLException {
        return dataSource.getConnection();
    }


    // Close the pool
    public static void closePool() {
        dataSource.close();
    }
}
```

Using **HikariCP** is much more efficient because it provides optimized connection pooling with non-blocking features and built-in connection validation. The connection pool is automatically managed, and it can scale well with increasing load.

Conclusion

In this chapter, you learned how to optimize performance in Java applications by identifying common performance bottlenecks and using strategies like **garbage collection tuning** and **connection pooling**. We explored the importance of **synchronization** to handle shared resources and prevent race conditions, and we looked at a practical example of optimizing a database connection pooling system.

By understanding performance optimization techniques, garbage collection, and using efficient libraries like **HikariCP** for connection pooling, you can significantly improve the performance and scalability of your Java applications. In the next chapters, we will explore additional performance-enhancing strategies such as **concurrency optimizations** and **multithreading best practices**.

Part 6

Java for Web Development

CHAPTER 19

INTRODUCTION TO WEB DEVELOPMENT WITH JAVA

Java and Web Development: An Overview of Java Technologies Used for Web Development

Java has a long history of being used for web development, providing robust, scalable, and secure technologies for building web applications. Several key Java technologies are commonly used in web development:

1. Java Servlet API

Java **Servlets** are server-side programs that handle requests from web browsers and generate dynamic web content, such as HTML pages. Servlets are Java classes that extend `HttpServlet` and are capable of processing HTTP requests (such as `GET`, `POST`, etc.) and returning HTTP responses. Servlets are the foundation for building Java-based web applications.

2. JavaServer Pages (JSP)

JavaServer Pages (JSP) is a technology used for developing dynamic web pages by embedding Java code directly into HTML. JSPs are often used in conjunction with Servlets to handle the business logic and view generation in web applications.

3. Java Frameworks

Several Java-based frameworks can help streamline the web development process:

- **Spring**: A comprehensive framework for building web applications, including tools for dependency injection, security, and data access.
- **JavaServer Faces (JSF)**: A component-based framework that simplifies the creation of user interfaces for web applications.

4. Web Servers and Containers

To run web applications in Java, you need a web server or servlet container. A **servlet container** provides the environment in which Servlets run and handles the HTTP requests. Popular servlet containers include:

- **Apache Tomcat**: A lightweight servlet container.

- **Jetty**: A more embedded, lightweight web server and servlet container.
- **WildFly (formerly JBoss)**: A full-featured application server for running Java EE applications.

In this chapter, we will focus on **Servlets**, which provide the building blocks for Java web development.

Setting Up a Basic Web Application Using Servlets

To create a basic web application in Java, we will need a servlet container (like Tomcat) to deploy and run our servlets. Let's break down the steps to set up a simple Java servlet-based web application.

Step 1: Install Apache Tomcat

1. **Download and Install**: Download Apache Tomcat from the official website (https://tomcat.apache.org/), and follow the installation instructions for your operating system.
2. **Configure the Server**: Once installed, you can configure the Tomcat server by editing the `conf/server.xml` file, though for most basic applications, the default configuration will be sufficient.

Step 2: Create the Web Application Directory Structure

A simple servlet-based web application follows this directory structure:

pgsql

```
/MyWebApp
    /WEB-INF
        web.xml
    /index.jsp
    /LoginServlet.java
```

- WEB-INF/ contains configuration files like web.xml and other resources that should not be directly accessible via the web browser.
- web.xml is the deployment descriptor that maps servlets to URLs and configures the servlet container.
- index.jsp is the JSP file that serves as the entry point of the application.
- LoginServlet.java is the Java class that handles user login.

Step 3: Write the web.xml Deployment Descriptor

The web.xml file defines the servlet and maps it to a specific URL pattern. Here's an example configuration for a login servlet:

xml

```xml
<?xml version="1.0" encoding="UTF-8"?>
<web-app
xmlns="http://java.sun.com/xml/ns/javaee"

xmlns:xsi="http://www.w3.org/2001/XMLSchema-
instance"

xsi:schemaLocation="http://java.sun.com/xml/ns/
javaee

http://java.sun.com/xml/ns/javaee/web-
app_3_1.xsd"
          version="3.1">
    <servlet>
        <servlet-name>LoginServlet</servlet-
name>
        <servlet-class>LoginServlet</servlet-
class>
    </servlet>
    <servlet-mapping>
        <servlet-name>LoginServlet</servlet-
name>
        <url-pattern>/login</url-pattern>
    </servlet-mapping>
</web-app>
```

This configuration tells the servlet container to map the `LoginServlet` class to the `/login` URL pattern.

Practical Example: A Simple Servlet-Based Application to Handle User Login

Let's now implement a simple login servlet that handles user login requests.

Step 1: Create the `LoginServlet.java`

java

```
import java.io.*;
import javax.servlet.*;
import javax.servlet.http.*;

public class LoginServlet extends HttpServlet {
    protected void doPost(HttpServletRequest request, HttpServletResponse response) throws ServletException, IOException {
        // Retrieve username and password from the form
        String username = request.getParameter("username");
        String password = request.getParameter("password");
```

226

```
        // Simulate a simple login check (in real
applications, use a database)
        if     ("user".equals(username)     &&
"password123".equals(password)) {
            // Redirect to a success page if
login is successful

response.sendRedirect("loginSuccess.jsp");
        } else {
            // Redirect to a failure page if
login fails

response.sendRedirect("loginFailure.jsp");
        }
    }
}
```

- The `LoginServlet` class extends `HttpServlet` and overrides the `doPost()` method to handle login form submissions.
- The `request.getParameter()` method is used to retrieve the username and password sent from the login form.

Step 2: Create the `index.jsp` File (Login Form)

jsp

```
<!DOCTYPE html>
<html>
```

227

```
<head>
    <title>Login Page</title>
</head>
<body>
    <h2>Login</h2>
    <form action="login" method="post">
        Username:      <input      type="text"
name="username"><br>
        Password:      <input      type="password"
name="password"><br>
        <input type="submit" value="Login">
    </form>
</body>
</html>
```

- The `index.jsp` file contains a simple HTML form where users can enter their username and password. The form uses the POST method to send the data to the LoginServlet.

Step 3: Create the Success and Failure Pages

1. **loginSuccess.jsp**: This page is displayed when the login is successful.

jsp

```
<!DOCTYPE html>
<html>
```

```
<head>
    <title>Login Success</title>
</head>
<body>
    <h2>Welcome, you have successfully logged
in!</h2>
</body>
</html>
```

2. **loginFailure.jsp**: This page is displayed when the login fails.

jsp

```
<!DOCTYPE html>
<html>
<head>
    <title>Login Failed</title>
</head>
<body>
    <h2>Login failed. Please check your username
and password and try again.</h2>
</body>
</html>
```

Step 4: Deploy the Application

1. **Compile the Java Class**: You can compile the servlet class using `javac` and deploy it in the `WEB-INF/classes` directory of the application.

2. **Start the Tomcat Server**: After deploying the application, start your Tomcat server by navigating to the `bin` directory and running `startup.sh` (on Linux/macOS) or `startup.bat` (on Windows).

3. **Access the Application**: Open your web browser and go to `http://localhost:8080/MyWebApp/` to access the login form.

Conclusion

In this chapter, we explored how to set up a simple Java web application using **Servlets**, a core technology for building web applications in Java. You learned about the **web.xml** configuration file and how to map a servlet to a URL pattern, as well as how to handle user input in a servlet and respond with appropriate pages.

By implementing a basic login system using a servlet, you gained hands-on experience in handling HTTP requests and responses, building web applications with Java, and using JSP for view generation.

In the next chapters, we will explore more advanced web development topics, including using **JavaServer Pages (JSP)** and **Java frameworks** like **Spring MVC** to further streamline the development process.

CHAPTER 20

JAVA SERVER PAGES (JSP) AND SERVLETS

Understanding JSP: Dynamic Content Generation for Web Applications

JavaServer Pages (JSP) is a technology used to develop dynamic web pages in Java. It allows Java code to be embedded directly into HTML using special tags. JSP files are compiled into servlets by the web container (e.g., Tomcat) before they are executed, so they combine the best of both worlds: dynamic content generation (like a servlet) and a simplified HTML-based interface.

1. The Basics of JSP

JSP enables you to write the presentation layer of a web application by embedding Java code within HTML tags. JSP is typically used to generate dynamic content like user interfaces, and it supports a clean separation between the logic (business layer) and presentation (view layer) of an application.

JSP Syntax:

232

- **Directives**: Provide information to the servlet container, such as page settings and imports.
- **Declarations**: Declare variables and methods in the page.
- **Scriptlets**: Contain Java code that is executed when the page is requested.
- **Expressions**: Output the result of Java code to the HTML response.
- **Tags**: Special tags like `<jsp:useBean>`, `<jsp:setProperty>`, and `<jsp:getProperty>` for working with JavaBeans.

Example of a JSP Page:

```jsp
<%@ page language="java" contentType="text/html;
charset=ISO-8859-1"%>
<html>
<head>
    <title>Welcome Page</title>
</head>
<body>
    <h2>Welcome to the user profile page!</h2>
    <p>Hello,                              <%=
request.getParameter("username") %>!</p>
</body>
</html>
```

- `<%@ page %>`: Directive that defines page attributes like language and content type.
- `<%= ... %>`: Scriptlet that prints the result of Java code to the response.

JSP helps separate the business logic (often handled by servlets) from the presentation (HTML and Java code for dynamic content), making it easier to manage the application and maintain a clean architecture.

The Role of Servlets in Java Web Development

While **JSP** is focused on generating the view layer of web applications, **Servlets** are responsible for processing requests and providing the underlying logic. A servlet is a Java class that runs on a web server, handling HTTP requests from clients (usually browsers) and generating HTTP responses.

Servlets and JSPs often work together in a web application, with servlets handling business logic and JSPs managing the presentation layer.

1. Servlet Overview

- **Request Handling**: A servlet receives HTTP requests from clients and generates responses.

- **Session Management**: Servlets manage user sessions (using `HttpSession`).
- **Database Interaction**: Servlets often interact with databases to retrieve or store data for dynamic web pages.

2. Servlet Life Cycle

The life cycle of a servlet consists of the following phases:

1. **Initialization**: The servlet container loads the servlet and initializes it using the `init()` method.
2. **Request Handling**: The servlet receives requests via the `service()` method, which processes HTTP requests (such as `doGet()`, `doPost()`, etc.).
3. **Destruction**: When the servlet is no longer needed, the container calls the `destroy()` method to clean up resources.

3. Servlet vs. JSP

- **Servlets** handle the logic of the web application, such as business rules and processing user requests.
- **JSP** is used for the presentation of the data, including generating dynamic content like HTML, JavaScript, and CSS.

Practical Example: Creating a Dynamic Web Page to Display User Profiles

Let's create a simple web application that displays a user profile using both **JSP** and **Servlets**. In this example, the servlet will handle the business logic of retrieving the user's data (such as username and email), and the JSP will render the dynamic content in the browser.

Step 1: Create the User Profile Servlet

The servlet will handle the logic of retrieving user data and forwarding the information to the JSP.

```java
import javax.servlet.*;
import javax.servlet.http.*;
import java.io.*;

public class UserProfileServlet extends HttpServlet {
    protected void doGet(HttpServletRequest request, HttpServletResponse response) throws ServletException, IOException {
        // Sample user data (in a real-world application, this data might come from a database)
        String username = "john_doe";
```

```
        String email = "john.doe@example.com";

        // Set the user data as request
attributes
        request.setAttribute("username",
username);
        request.setAttribute("email", email);

        // Forward the request to the JSP page
for rendering
        RequestDispatcher        dispatcher       =
request.getRequestDispatcher("userProfile.jsp")
;
        dispatcher.forward(request, response);
    }
}
```

Explanation:

- The `doGet()` method retrieves user data (in this case, hardcoded) and stores it in request attributes.
- The `RequestDispatcher` forwards the request and data to the `userProfile.jsp` page for rendering.

Step 2: Create the `userProfile.jsp` Page

The JSP page will display the user's profile dynamically based on the data passed by the servlet.

```
jsp
```

```
<%@ page language="java" contentType="text/html;
charset=ISO-8859-1"%>
<html>
<head>
    <title>User Profile</title>
</head>
<body>
    <h2>User Profile</h2>
    <p>Username:                        <%=
request.getAttribute("username") %></p>
    <p>Email: <%= request.getAttribute("email")
%></p>
</body>
</html>
```

Explanation:

- The `request.getAttribute()` method is used to retrieve the user data passed from the servlet.
- The JSP then renders this data in HTML format, dynamically displaying the username and email.

Step 3: Configure the `web.xml` File

In the `web.xml` deployment descriptor, we need to define the servlet and map it to a specific URL pattern.

xml

```xml
<?xml version="1.0" encoding="UTF-8"?>
<web-app
xmlns="http://java.sun.com/xml/ns/javaee"

xmlns:xsi="http://www.w3.org/2001/XMLSchema-
instance"

xsi:schemaLocation="http://java.sun.com/xml/ns/
javaee

http://java.sun.com/xml/ns/javaee/web-
app_3_1.xsd"
        version="3.1">
    <servlet>
        <servlet-
name>UserProfileServlet</servlet-name>
        <servlet-
class>UserProfileServlet</servlet-class>
    </servlet>
    <servlet-mapping>
        <servlet-
name>UserProfileServlet</servlet-name>
        <url-pattern>/userProfile</url-pattern>
    </servlet-mapping>
</web-app>
```

Explanation:

- The servlet UserProfileServlet is mapped to the
  URL pattern /userProfile, meaning it will handle

239

requests   to   `http://localhost:8080/your-`
`webapp/userProfile`.

Step 4: Deploy and Test the Application

1. **Deploy the Application**:
   - Place the compiled servlet class in the `WEB-INF/classes` directory.
   - Ensure the `userProfile.jsp` page is in the root directory or `WEB-INF` directory (depending on the project structure).
   - Deploy the application to your servlet container (e.g., Apache Tomcat).

2. **Test the Application**:
   - Open a web browser and navigate to `http://localhost:8080/your-webapp/userProfile` to see the dynamically generated user profile page.

Conclusion

In this chapter, you learned how to combine **Java Servlets** and **JavaServer Pages (JSP)** to create dynamic web applications. Servlets are used for handling requests, processing business logic, and managing data, while JSP is used for generating the dynamic content on the view layer.

By developing a simple user profile application, you saw how servlets and JSP work together to provide a clean separation of concerns in a web application. The servlet handles data retrieval and business logic, while the JSP is responsible for rendering the view.

In the next chapters, we will explore more advanced web development topics such as **Session Management**, **Java Frameworks (Spring MVC)**, and **RESTful Web Services** to enhance your skills in building Java-based web applications.

241

CHAPTER 21

INTRODUCTION TO JAVA SPRING FRAMEWORK

Why Spring? Understanding the Spring Ecosystem and Its Advantages

The **Spring Framework** is a powerful, flexible, and comprehensive framework for building Java-based applications. It provides a wide range of capabilities, including support for dependency injection, aspect-oriented programming, transaction management, and more. It also supports creating modern enterprise applications like microservices, web applications, and REST APIs.

1. What is the Spring Framework?

Spring is an open-source framework that simplifies the development of Java applications by providing a comprehensive programming and configuration model. It consists of several modules that can be used independently or together. Key components of the Spring ecosystem include:

- **Core Container**: The core features of Spring, including Dependency Injection (DI) and Aspect-Oriented Programming (AOP).

- **Spring MVC**: A web framework for building web applications using the Model-View-Controller (MVC) design pattern.

- **Spring Data**: A set of tools for working with databases and simplifying data access.

- **Spring Security**: A powerful and customizable framework for securing applications.

- **Spring Boot**: A module that simplifies the configuration and deployment of Spring applications.

2. Why Choose Spring?

- **Inversion of Control (IoC)**: Spring uses the IoC pattern to manage object creation and dependency injection. This helps reduce coupling between components and makes the system easier to test and maintain.

- **Aspect-Oriented Programming (AOP)**: Spring provides support for AOP, allowing you to separate cross-cutting concerns (like logging, security, or transaction management) from your core business logic.

- **Flexible Configuration**: Spring allows you to configure your application through XML, annotations, or Java-based configuration, making it adaptable to different needs.

243

- **Modularity**: Spring's modular architecture allows you to use only the parts you need, which reduces overhead and complexity.

- **Spring Boot**: Simplifies application setup, providing out-of-the-box configurations and minimal setup requirements to quickly get started with Spring-based applications.

3. The Spring Ecosystem

- **Spring Core**: Provides fundamental features such as IoC and DI.

- **Spring Boot**: Simplifies the setup and configuration of Spring applications, making it ideal for microservices and stand-alone applications.

- **Spring Cloud**: Provides tools for building cloud-native applications, with features like service discovery, configuration management, and circuit breakers.

- **Spring Data**: Offers a consistent model for accessing different types of databases (SQL, NoSQL).

- **Spring Security**: Provides robust security features, including authentication, authorization, and encryption.

Setting Up a Spring Boot Application for Building Microservices

Spring Boot is a popular choice for developing microservices because it simplifies the configuration and deployment of Spring applications. It allows you to quickly build standalone, production-ready applications with minimal configuration. Spring Boot applications are typically packaged as **JAR** (Java ARchive) files or **WAR** (Web Application Archive) files and can be easily deployed to any environment, including local machines, cloud services, or containerized environments.

1. What is Spring Boot?

Spring Boot is an extension of the Spring Framework that simplifies the development of Spring applications. It provides:

- **Automatic Configuration**: Spring Boot automatically configures your application based on the libraries in your classpath.
- **Embedded Web Servers**: Spring Boot comes with embedded web servers like Tomcat, Jetty, and Undertow, which means you don't need to deploy your application to a separate web server.
- **Production-Ready Features**: Spring Boot provides out-of-the-box features for monitoring, health checks, and metrics, which are essential for microservices.
- **Minimal Setup**: Spring Boot minimizes the amount of configuration required to get your application up and running.

245

2. Setting Up Spring Boot

To set up a Spring Boot application, you can use the Spring Initializr (https://start.spring.io/), which provides a web interface to generate the basic structure of a Spring Boot project. Alternatively, you can use your favorite IDE (like IntelliJ IDEA or Eclipse) to create a Spring Boot project.

- **Step 1**: Open Spring Initializr and choose the following options:
    - o **Project**: Maven Project (or Gradle, depending on your preference)
    - o **Language**: Java
    - o **Spring Boot Version**: Select the latest stable version
    - o **Group**: com.example
    - o **Artifact**: mymicroservice
    - o **Dependencies**: Add `Spring Web`, `Spring Boot DevTools`, `Spring Data JPA`, and any other dependencies as needed.
- **Step 2**: Download the generated project and import it into your IDE.
- **Step 3**: Create a main application class with the `@SpringBootApplication` annotation to bootstrap the application.

Practical Example: Developing a Simple RESTful API with Spring Boot

Let's create a simple **RESTful API** that handles user data using Spring Boot. This API will allow us to:

1. Add a new user.
2. Retrieve user information by ID.

Step 1: Define the User Model

Create a class User that will represent the user data.

```java
package com.example.mymicroservice.model;

public class User {
    private Long id;
    private String name;
    private String email;

    // Getters and Setters

    public User(Long id, String name, String email) {
        this.id = id;
        this.name = name;
        this.email = email;
```

```java
    }

    // Getters and Setters
    public Long getId() {
        return id;
    }

    public void setId(Long id) {
        this.id = id;
    }

    public String getName() {
        return name;
    }

    public void setName(String name) {
        this.name = name;
    }

    public String getEmail() {
        return email;
    }

    public void setEmail(String email) {
        this.email = email;
    }
}
```

Step 2: Create a Controller to Handle RESTful Requests

Create a controller class that will handle HTTP requests to manage users.

```java
package com.example.mymicroservice.controller;

import com.example.mymicroservice.model.User;
import org.springframework.web.bind.annotation.*;

import java.util.HashMap;
import java.util.Map;

@RestController
@RequestMapping("/users")
public class UserController {
    private Map<Long, User> userDatabase = new HashMap<>();

    // Endpoint to create a user
    @PostMapping
    public User createUser(@RequestBody User user) {
        user.setId((long) (userDatabase.size() + 1)); // Simple ID generation logic
        userDatabase.put(user.getId(), user);
```

```
        return user;
    }


    // Endpoint to get a user by ID
    @GetMapping("/{id}")
    public User getUser(@PathVariable Long id) {
        return userDatabase.get(id);
    }
}
```

In this controller:

- **@RestController**: This annotation indicates that the class is a REST controller, and the response from each method will be automatically serialized to JSON or XML.
- **@RequestMapping("/users")**: This specifies the base URL for all user-related endpoints.
- **@PostMapping**: Handles HTTP POST requests to create a user.
- **@GetMapping("/{id}")**: Handles HTTP GET requests to retrieve a user by ID.

Step 3: Running the Spring Boot Application

Create a `main` application class that contains the `@SpringBootApplication` annotation, which serves as the entry point for the application.

```java

package com.example.mymicroservice;

import
org.springframework.boot.SpringApplication;
import
org.springframework.boot.autoconfigure.SpringBo
otApplication;

@SpringBootApplication
public class MyMicroserviceApplication {
    public static void main(String[] args) {

SpringApplication.run(MyMicroserviceApplication
.class, args);
    }
}
```

- **@SpringBootApplication**: This annotation marks the main entry point of the Spring Boot application and enables automatic configuration, component scanning, and more.

Step 4: Test the API Using Postman

Now that the application is set up, we can test the RESTful API using Postman or any other API testing tool.

1. **Create a User**:

    o Send a **POST** request to
       `http://localhost:8080/users` with a
       JSON body:

```json
json

{

    "name": "John Doe",
    "email": "johndoe@example.com"
}
```

2. **Get a User**:

    o Send a **GET** request to
       `http://localhost:8080/users/1` to
       retrieve the user information by ID.

Conclusion

In this chapter, you learned about the **Spring Framework** and its advantages for building modern Java-based applications, including web applications and microservices. We explored **Spring Boot**, which simplifies application setup and configuration, and developed a simple **RESTful API** using Spring Boot.

Through the practical example of creating a user management system, you saw how easy it is to build a web service with Spring Boot, using controllers to handle HTTP requests and responses.

In the next chapters, we will explore more advanced Spring concepts, including **Spring Security**, **Spring Data**, and **Spring Cloud**, to enhance the functionality and scalability of your applications.

Part 7

Exploring Data and Database Integration

CHAPTER 22

JAVA DATABASE CONNECTIVITY (JDBC)

Introduction to JDBC: Connecting Java Applications with Relational Databases

Java Database Connectivity (JDBC) is a Java API that allows Java applications to interact with relational databases using SQL (Structured Query Language). JDBC provides a standard interface for connecting to databases, executing queries, and retrieving results. It is part of the **Java SE** (Standard Edition) platform and is widely used in Java applications for data management.

1. What is JDBC?

JDBC provides a set of classes and interfaces that enable Java programs to:

- **Establish a Connection**: Connect to a relational database using a database driver.
- **Execute SQL Queries**: Run SQL commands like SELECT, INSERT, UPDATE, and DELETE.

255

- **Process Results**: Handle the results returned by SQL queries (such as retrieving data or updating records).
- **Handle Exceptions**: Handle SQL errors and other database-related issues.

2. JDBC Architecture

JDBC works by using a **driver-based architecture**, where:

- **JDBC Drivers**: JDBC uses different database drivers to establish a connection with the database. Each relational database (like MySQL, PostgreSQL, Oracle, etc.) requires a specific JDBC driver.
- **Connection**: The `Connection` object represents an open connection to a database. It is used to create `Statement` objects for executing SQL queries.
- **Statement**: A `Statement` is used to execute SQL queries against the database.
- **ResultSet**: A `ResultSet` is used to retrieve the data returned by a `SELECT` query.

JDBC is also flexible in that it supports **different types of database drivers**:

- **Type-1 Driver (JDBC-ODBC bridge)**: Uses ODBC (Open Database Connectivity) to connect to the database.

- **Type-2 Driver (Native-API driver)**: Uses a native database API to connect to the database.

- **Type-3 Driver (Network Protocol driver)**: Uses a database-independent protocol to communicate with the database.

- **Type-4 Driver (Thin driver)**: Directly communicates with the database using the database's native protocol.

Performing CRUD Operations: Using SQL to Interact with Databases

The most common operations you will perform when interacting with a database through JDBC are **CRUD** operations: **Create**, **Read**, **Update**, and **Delete**. Let's review how to perform each of these operations using SQL and JDBC.

1. Create Operation (INSERT)

The INSERT SQL command is used to add new records to a database table.

Example SQL Query:

sql

```
INSERT INTO employees (id, name, department)
VALUES (1, 'Alice', 'Engineering');
```

257

In JDBC, you would use a `Statement` or `PreparedStatement` object to execute this query.

2. Read Operation (SELECT)

The `SELECT` SQL command is used to retrieve data from a database.

Example SQL Query:

sql

```sql
SELECT * FROM employees WHERE department = 'Engineering';
```

In JDBC, you would execute a `SELECT` query and process the `ResultSet` to retrieve the data.

3. Update Operation (UPDATE)

The `UPDATE` SQL command is used to modify existing records in a database.

Example SQL Query:

sql

```sql
UPDATE employees SET department = 'HR' WHERE id = 1;
```

4. Delete Operation (DELETE)

The DELETE SQL command is used to remove records from a database.

Example SQL Query:

```sql
sql
```

```sql
DELETE FROM employees WHERE id = 1;
```

Practical Example: Building a Simple Inventory Management System Using JDBC

Let's build a simple **inventory management system** using JDBC. We'll create a database table to store product information (like product ID, name, and quantity), and implement CRUD operations to add, view, update, and delete products.

Step 1: Setting Up the Database

First, we need to create the database and the products table. You can use MySQL or any other relational database.

Create Database:

```sql
sql
```

259

```sql
CREATE DATABASE inventory;
```

Create Table:

sql

```sql
CREATE TABLE products (
    id INT AUTO_INCREMENT PRIMARY KEY,
    name VARCHAR(100),
    quantity INT
);
```

Step 2: Establishing the JDBC Connection

We'll now set up the connection to the database using JDBC. Make sure you have the appropriate JDBC driver (for MySQL, you need the `mysql-connector-java` driver).

java

```java
import java.sql.Connection;
import java.sql.DriverManager;
import java.sql.SQLException;

public class DatabaseConnection {
    public static Connection getConnection() {
        try {
            // Load and register the JDBC driver
(for MySQL)
```

```
Class.forName("com.mysql.cj.jdbc.Driver");

        // Establish the connection to the
database
        return
DriverManager.getConnection("jdbc:mysql://local
host:3306/inventory", "root", "password");
    } catch (ClassNotFoundException |
SQLException e) {
        e.printStackTrace();
    }
    return null;
  }
}
```

This code loads the MySQL JDBC driver and establishes a connection to the database.

Step 3: Implementing CRUD Operations

1. **Create Product (INSERT)**

```java

import java.sql.Connection;
import java.sql.PreparedStatement;
import java.sql.SQLException;

public class ProductDAO {
```

```java
// Insert product into the database
public void createProduct(String name, int quantity) {
    String query = "INSERT INTO products (name, quantity) VALUES (?, ?)";

    try (Connection connection = DatabaseConnection.getConnection();
        PreparedStatement statement = connection.prepareStatement(query)) {

        statement.setString(1, name);
        statement.setInt(2, quantity);
        statement.executeUpdate();
        System.out.println("Product added successfully.");
    } catch (SQLException e) {
        e.printStackTrace();
    }
}
}
```

2. Read Product (SELECT)

java

```java
import java.sql.*;

public class ProductDAO {
    // Retrieve product by ID
```

```java
    public void getProduct(int id) {
        String query = "SELECT * FROM products
WHERE id = ?";

        try (Connection connection =
DatabaseConnection.getConnection();
            PreparedStatement statement =
connection.prepareStatement(query)) {

            statement.setInt(1, id);
            ResultSet resultSet =
statement.executeQuery();

            if (resultSet.next()) {
                String name =
resultSet.getString("name");
                int quantity =
resultSet.getInt("quantity");
                System.out.println("Product ID:
" + id + ", Name: " + name + ", Quantity: " +
quantity);
            } else {
                System.out.println("Product not
found.");
            }
        } catch (SQLException e) {
            e.printStackTrace();
        }
    }
```

}

3. Update Product (UPDATE)

java

```java
import java.sql.*;

public class ProductDAO {
    // Update product quantity by ID
    public void updateProduct(int id, int quantity) {
        String query = "UPDATE products SET quantity = ? WHERE id = ?";

        try (Connection connection = DatabaseConnection.getConnection();
             PreparedStatement statement = connection.prepareStatement(query)) {

            statement.setInt(1, quantity);
            statement.setInt(2, id);
            statement.executeUpdate();
            System.out.println("Product updated successfully.");
        } catch (SQLException e) {
            e.printStackTrace();
        }
    }
}
```

4. Delete Product (DELETE)

java

```java
import java.sql.*;

public class ProductDAO {
    // Delete product by ID
    public void deleteProduct(int id) {
        String query = "DELETE FROM products WHERE id = ?";

        try (Connection connection = DatabaseConnection.getConnection();
            PreparedStatement statement = connection.prepareStatement(query)) {

            statement.setInt(1, id);
            statement.executeUpdate();
            System.out.println("Product deleted successfully.");
        } catch (SQLException e) {
            e.printStackTrace();
        }
    }
}
```

Step 4: Testing the Application

Finally, let's create a simple `main()` method to test the CRUD operations.

java

```java
public class InventoryApp {
    public static void main(String[] args) {
        ProductDAO        productDAO      =      new
ProductDAO();

        // Create a new product
        productDAO.createProduct("Laptop", 10);

        // Get product by ID
        productDAO.getProduct(1);

        // Update product quantity
        productDAO.updateProduct(1, 15);

        // Delete product
        productDAO.deleteProduct(1);
    }
}
```

Conclusion

In this chapter, you learned how to use **Java Database Connectivity (JDBC)** to connect a Java application with a relational database. You saw how to perform **CRUD operations** (Create, Read, Update, Delete) using SQL and JDBC, and how to manage data using `Connection`, `PreparedStatement`, and `ResultSet` objects.

Through the practical example of building a simple inventory management system, you saw how to interact with a MySQL database, handle SQL exceptions, and perform basic database operations. JDBC remains a core technology for accessing and manipulating data in relational databases in Java applications.

In the next chapters, we will explore more advanced database integration techniques, including **using Java Persistence API (JPA)** and **Spring Data JPA** for easier data management in modern Java applications.

CHAPTER 23

OBJECT-RELATIONAL MAPPING (ORM) WITH HIBERNATE

Understanding ORM: How Hibernate Simplifies Database Interaction

Object-Relational Mapping (ORM) is a technique that allows you to map Java objects to database tables and vice versa, providing a bridge between the object-oriented world of Java and the relational world of SQL databases. ORM tools handle the boilerplate code required for database operations, such as inserting, updating, and deleting records, allowing developers to focus on the business logic of the application rather than dealing with low-level database operations.

Hibernate is one of the most popular ORM frameworks for Java. It provides a set of tools that allows Java applications to interact with databases using object-oriented paradigms, eliminating the need for manual SQL queries in most cases. Hibernate automates many tasks, such as mapping Java classes to database tables, managing the persistence of Java objects, and handling transaction management.

1. Advantages of Using Hibernate

- **Simplified Data Persistence**: Hibernate abstracts away the complexities of database interaction, allowing you to work with objects rather than writing SQL queries for every CRUD (Create, Read, Update, Delete) operation.

- **Automatic SQL Generation**: Hibernate generates the necessary SQL statements behind the scenes, based on the object model.

- **Database Independence**: Hibernate abstracts database interactions, allowing your application to be easily portable between different databases.

- **Lazy Loading**: Hibernate supports lazy loading, meaning data is fetched only when it is required, improving performance.

- **Caching**: Hibernate offers first-level and second-level caching mechanisms that reduce the need for repetitive database queries, further improving performance.

Setting Up Hibernate: Connecting Your Java Application to a Database Using Hibernate

Setting up Hibernate involves configuring your Java application to use Hibernate as the ORM framework. Hibernate uses a configuration file called **hibernate.cfg.xml** for database

269

connection details and mapping classes. In addition, entity classes must be annotated with Hibernate-specific annotations to define the mapping between the object and database.

1. Steps to Set Up Hibernate

Here are the steps to set up Hibernate in your Java application:

Step 1: Add Hibernate and Database Dependencies

If you are using Maven, add the following dependencies to your pom.xml to include Hibernate and your database driver (e.g., MySQL driver):

xml

```xml
<dependencies>
    <!-- Hibernate Core Dependency -->
    <dependency>
        <groupId>org.hibernate</groupId>
        <artifactId>hibernate-core</artifactId>
        <version>5.5.7.Final</version>
    </dependency>
    <!-- MySQL Driver Dependency -->
    <dependency>
        <groupId>mysql</groupId>
        <artifactId>mysql-connector-
java</artifactId>
        <version>8.0.26</version>
```

```
    </dependency>
</dependencies>
```

Step 2: Configure Hibernate Using `hibernate.cfg.xml`

Create a configuration file named `hibernate.cfg.xml` in the `src/main/resources` folder to provide Hibernate with information about the database connection and other settings.

xml

```xml
<?xml version="1.0" encoding="UTF-8"?>
<!DOCTYPE hibernate-configuration PUBLIC "-
//Hibernate/Hibernate Configuration DTD 3.0//EN"
"http://hibernate.sourceforge.net/hibernate-
configuration-3.0.dtd">
<hibernate-configuration>
    <session-factory>
        <!-- JDBC Database connection settings -
->
        <property
name="hibernate.dialect">org.hibernate.dialect.
MySQLDialect</property>
        <property
name="hibernate.driver_class">com.mysql.cj.jdbc
.Driver</property>
        <property
name="hibernate.url">jdbc:mysql://localhost:330
6/your_database</property>
```

271

```xml
        <property
name="hibernate.username">root</property>
        <property
name="hibernate.password">password</property>


        <!-- JDBC connection pool settings -->
        <property
name="hibernate.c3p0.min_size">5</property>
        <property
name="hibernate.c3p0.max_size">20</property>
        <property
name="hibernate.c3p0.timeout">300</property>
        <property
name="hibernate.c3p0.max_statements">50</proper
ty>
        <property
name="hibernate.c3p0.idle_test_period">3000</pr
operty>


        <!-- Specify the JDBC driver -->
        <property
name="hibernate.connection.pool_size">10</prope
rty>


        <!--   Enable   Hibernate's   automatic
session context management -->
        <property
name="hibernate.current_session_context_class">
thread</property>
```

```
<!-- Echo all executed SQL to stdout -->
<property
name="hibernate.show_sql">true</property>

<!-- Drop and re-create the database
schema on startup -->
<property
name="hibernate.hbm2ddl.auto">update</property>

<!-- Mention annotated class -->
<mapping
class="com.example.model.Customer"/>
</session-factory>
</hibernate-configuration>
```

- **`hibernate.dialect`**: Specifies the SQL dialect for the specific database (e.g., MySQL).
- **`hibernate.url`,   `hibernate.username`, `hibernate.password`**: Database connection details.
- **`hibernate.hbm2ddl.auto`**: Defines how Hibernate should manage the database schema. Use `update` to automatically update the schema based on the entity classes.

Step 3: Create Entity Classes

Create Java classes that will be persisted in the database. Use Hibernate annotations to map the class properties to database table columns.

```java
package com.example.model;

import javax.persistence.Entity;
import javax.persistence.GeneratedValue;
import javax.persistence.GenerationType;
import javax.persistence.Id;

@Entity
public class Customer {
    @Id
    @GeneratedValue(strategy            =
GenerationType.IDENTITY)
    private int id;
    private String name;
    private String email;

    // Constructor, getters, and setters
    public Customer() {}

    public Customer(String name, String email) {
        this.name = name;
        this.email = email;
    }
```

```java
// Getters and Setters
public int getId() {
    return id;
}

public void setId(int id) {
    this.id = id;
}

public String getName() {
    return name;
}

public void setName(String name) {
    this.name = name;
}

public String getEmail() {
    return email;
}

public void setEmail(String email) {
    this.email = email;
}
}
```

- **@Entity**: Specifies that this class will be persisted in the database.

275

- **@Id**: Marks the primary key field.

- **@GeneratedValue**: Specifies the strategy for generating primary key values.

Practical Example: A Hibernate-based Application to Manage Customer Orders

Let's create a simple Hibernate-based application to manage customer orders. The application will allow you to perform CRUD operations for customers.

Step 1: Define the Order Entity

In addition to the Customer entity, we will define an Order entity.

java

```java
package com.example.model;

import javax.persistence.Entity;
import javax.persistence.GeneratedValue;
import javax.persistence.GenerationType;
import javax.persistence.Id;

@Entity
public class Order {
```

```java
    @Id
    @GeneratedValue(strategy                    =
GenerationType.IDENTITY)
    private int id;
    private String productName;
    private int quantity;
    private double price;

    // Constructor, getters, and setters
    public Order() {}

    public    Order(String    productName,    int
quantity, double price) {
        this.productName = productName;
        this.quantity = quantity;
        this.price = price;
    }

    // Getters and Setters
    public int getId() {
        return id;
    }

    public void setId(int id) {
        this.id = id;
    }

    public String getProductName() {
        return productName;
```

```
    }

    public       void        setProductName(String
productName) {
        this.productName = productName;
    }

    public int getQuantity() {
        return quantity;
    }

    public void setQuantity(int quantity) {
        this.quantity = quantity;
    }

    public double getPrice() {
        return price;
    }

    public void setPrice(double price) {
        this.price = price;
    }
}
```

Step 2: Create a Hibernate Utility Class

This class will help in creating and managing Hibernate sessions.

```
java
```

```java
package com.example.util;

import org.hibernate.Session;
import org.hibernate.SessionFactory;
import org.hibernate.cfg.Configuration;

public class HibernateUtil {
    private static SessionFactory sessionFactory;

    static {
        // Build the SessionFactory based on the configuration
        sessionFactory = new Configuration().configure("hibernate.cfg.xml").addAnnotatedClass(Customer.class)

.addAnnotatedClass(Order.class).buildSessionFactory();
    }

    public static Session getSession() {
        return sessionFactory.getCurrentSession();
    }

    public static void closeSessionFactory() {
        sessionFactory.close();
    }
```

}

Step 3: Performing CRUD Operations

Now, let's implement the CRUD operations for managing customers and orders.

1. Create Customer

java

```java
public class CustomerService {
    public void createCustomer(String name,
String email) {
        Session session =
HibernateUtil.getSession();
        try {
            // Start a transaction
            session.beginTransaction();

            // Create a new customer object
            Customer customer = new
Customer(name, email);

            // Save the customer
            session.save(customer);

            // Commit the transaction
            session.getTransaction().commit();
        } finally {
```

```
HibernateUtil.closeSessionFactory();
        }
    }
}
```

2. Create Order

java

```java
public class OrderService {
    public void createOrder(int customerId,
String productName, int quantity, double price)
{
        Session session =
HibernateUtil.getSession();
        try {
            session.beginTransaction();

            // Get the customer by ID
            Customer customer =
session.get(Customer.class, customerId);

            // Create a new order and associate
it with the customer
            Order order = new Order(productName,
quantity, price);
            customer.getOrders().add(order); //
Assuming a one-to-many relationship
```

281

```
    // Save the order
    session.save(order);

        session.getTransaction().commit();
    } finally {

HibernateUtil.closeSessionFactory();
    }
  }
}
```

Conclusion

In this chapter, you learned about **Object-Relational Mapping (ORM)** and how Hibernate simplifies database interactions in Java applications. Hibernate handles many tasks for you, such as mapping Java objects to database tables and automating SQL query generation, allowing you to focus on business logic rather than database management.

Through the practical example of building an application to manage customer orders, you gained hands-on experience with Hibernate's powerful features, including entity mapping, session management, and CRUD operations.

In the next chapters, we will explore more advanced Hibernate concepts, including **relationship mappings, advanced queries,** and **transaction management** for building more complex and scalable applications.

Part 8

Java in the Real World

CHAPTER 24

BUILDING A SIMPLE DESKTOP APPLICATION IN JAVA

JavaFX Basics: Setting Up JavaFX for Desktop UI Development

JavaFX is a powerful framework for building desktop applications with rich graphical user interfaces (GUIs). It provides a set of UI controls, 2D and 3D graphics, media support, and many other features for creating modern desktop applications. JavaFX is the successor to **Swing**, offering a more modern and flexible way to develop cross-platform desktop applications in Java.

1. Why JavaFX?

- **Rich User Interfaces**: JavaFX provides a wide range of built-in UI controls like buttons, text fields, tables, charts, and more.
- **Scene Graph**: JavaFX uses a scene graph to organize the UI elements, which allows for efficient rendering of graphical content.

- **CSS Styling**: You can style JavaFX applications using CSS (Cascading Style Sheets), which enables you to create visually appealing UIs.
- **Cross-Platform**: JavaFX applications can run on various operating systems such as Windows, macOS, and Linux.

2. Setting Up JavaFX

To develop JavaFX applications, you need the following:

- **Java Development Kit (JDK)**: Ensure you have JDK 8 or above installed.
- **JavaFX SDK**: Since JavaFX is no longer bundled with JDK starting from JDK 11, you need to download the JavaFX SDK from the official website (https://openjfx.io/).
- **IDE Setup**: You can use IDEs like IntelliJ IDEA, Eclipse, or NetBeans, which have built-in support for JavaFX development.

For Maven-based projects, you can include the JavaFX dependencies in your pom.xml:

```xml
<dependencies>
    <dependency>
        <groupId>org.openjfx</groupId>
```

286

```
        <artifactId>javafx-
controls</artifactId>
        <version>16</version>
    </dependency>
    <dependency>
        <groupId>org.openjfx</groupId>
        <artifactId>javafx-fxml</artifactId>
        <version>16</version>
    </dependency>
</dependencies>
```

Make sure to configure your IDE to use the correct JDK and JavaFX libraries.

___

Event Handling: Making Your Application Interactive

Event handling in JavaFX allows your application to respond to user actions such as button clicks, key presses, mouse movements, and more. The JavaFX event model is built around the observer pattern, where events are generated by user actions and then passed to the appropriate event handler.

1. Basic Event Handling Flow:

- **Event Generation**: A user interacts with a UI control (e.g., a button), generating an event.

- **Event Handling**: The event is passed to an event handler (a method that processes the event).
- **Event Processing**: The event handler executes code to respond to the user's action, such as updating the UI or performing a task.

2. Types of Event Handlers:

- **Lambda Expressions**: Java 8+ allows you to use lambda expressions to handle events concisely.
- **Anonymous Classes**: You can also define event handlers using anonymous classes, though lambdas are more concise.

Example: Button Event Handler

java

```
Button button = new Button("Click Me");
button.setOnAction(e -> {
    System.out.println("Button was clicked!");
});
```

In this example:

- The setOnAction method registers an event handler for button clicks.
- The event handler uses a lambda expression to print a message to the console when the button is clicked.

Practical Example: A Simple Task Manager Application Using JavaFX

Now, let's build a **simple task manager** application using JavaFX. The application will allow users to:

- Add tasks.
- Display tasks in a list.
- Mark tasks as completed.

Step 1: Setting Up the JavaFX Application

We will start by creating the main application class that extends `Application` (the base class for JavaFX applications) and overrides the `start()` method to set up the UI components.

```java
import javafx.application.Application;
import javafx.scene.Scene;
import javafx.scene.control.*;
import javafx.scene.layout.VBox;
import javafx.stage.Stage;

public class TaskManagerApp extends Application
{
```

```java
@Override
public void start(Stage primaryStage) {
    // Create a TextField to input task
description
    TextField taskInput = new TextField();
    taskInput.setPromptText("Enter   a   new
task");

    // Create a ListView to display tasks
    ListView<String>   taskList   =   new
ListView<>();

    // Create a Button to add tasks
    Button   addButton   =   new   Button("Add
Task");

    // Add event handler to the button
    addButton.setOnAction(e -> {
        String task = taskInput.getText();
        if (!task.isEmpty()) {
            taskList.getItems().add(task);
// Add task to the list
            taskInput.clear();   // Clear the
input field
        }
    });

    // Create a Button to mark tasks as
completed
```

```java
        Button completeButton = new Button("Mark
as Completed");

        // Add event handler to the complete
button
        completeButton.setOnAction(e -> {
            String        selectedTask       =
taskList.getSelectionModel().getSelectedItem();
            if (selectedTask != null) {

taskList.getItems().remove(selectedTask);

taskList.getItems().add(selectedTask    +      "
(Completed)");
            }
        });

        // Layout the UI elements in a VBox
        VBox layout = new VBox(10, taskInput,
addButton, completeButton, taskList);

        // Set the scene and stage
        Scene scene = new Scene(layout, 400,
300);
        primaryStage.setTitle("Task Manager");
        primaryStage.setScene(scene);
        primaryStage.show();
    }
```

291

```
public static void main(String[] args) {
    launch(args);    // Launch the JavaFX
application
    }
}
```

Explanation of the Code:

- **TextField**: Used to input new tasks.
- **ListView**: Displays the list of tasks.
- **Button**: There are two buttons:
  - **Add Task**: Adds a task to the list.
  - **Mark as Completed**: Marks the selected task as completed by appending "(Completed)" to the task text and moving it to the bottom of the list.
- **Event Handlers**:
  - The `setOnAction()` method is used to assign event handlers to the buttons.
  - The `taskList.getSelectionModel().getSelectedItem()` method retrieves the selected task when marking it as completed.
- **VBox**: A vertical box layout is used to arrange the UI elements.

Step 2: Running the Application

When you run the application:

292

1. You can enter a task in the text field and click the **"Add Task"** button to add the task to the list.

2. You can select a task in the list and click the **"Mark as Completed"** button to mark the task as completed.

Conclusion

In this chapter, you learned how to build a **simple desktop application** using **JavaFX**. You explored how to create and handle **JavaFX UI controls** like buttons, text fields, and list views. Additionally, you saw how to implement **event handling** to make the application interactive and respond to user actions.

By developing a basic **task manager application**, you gained hands-on experience with JavaFX and its powerful UI features. JavaFX provides a great foundation for building modern, interactive desktop applications with Java, and this knowledge is essential for developing a wide range of desktop-based solutions.

In the next chapters, we will explore more advanced **JavaFX** topics, including custom UI controls, **FXML** (FXML for declarative UI), and how to use **JavaFX** with databases for more complex desktop applications.

CHAPTER 25

JAVA SECURITY AND BEST PRACTICES

Security in Java: Protecting Your Application from Common Security Threats

In today's interconnected world, security is a critical concern for every software application. Java provides several mechanisms to help you secure your applications from common threats like **data breaches**, **code injection**, **cross-site scripting (XSS)**, and **man-in-the-middle attacks**. Writing secure code not only protects your data and users but also helps ensure that your application remains trustworthy and reliable.

1. Common Security Threats in Java

- **SQL Injection**: This occurs when an attacker can manipulate an SQL query by injecting malicious input. It can lead to unauthorized access to a database.
- **Cross-Site Scripting (XSS)**: This attack allows attackers to inject malicious scripts into web pages, which can then be executed in the user's browser.

- **Cross-Site Request Forgery (CSRF)**: An attacker tricks a user into performing unwanted actions on a web application where they are authenticated.
- **Session Hijacking**: Attackers can steal session identifiers (cookies or tokens) to impersonate users.
- **Denial of Service (DoS)**: Attackers overwhelm a service by sending an excessive amount of requests, causing it to become unavailable.

2. Java Security Features

Java provides several built-in features and libraries to protect your application from security threats:

- **Java Security Manager**: Manages access to system resources and limits the operations that can be performed by Java applications.
- **Java Cryptography Architecture (JCA)**: A set of APIs for implementing cryptographic operations such as encryption, decryption, hashing, and digital signatures.
- **SSL/TLS**: Secure communication protocols for encrypting data over the network.
- **Authentication and Authorization**: Java provides frameworks like **JAAS (Java Authentication and Authorization Service)** to secure applications by managing user authentication and access control.

3. Protecting Data with Encryption and Hashing

For sensitive data, Java provides cryptographic tools to help with **encryption** (for protecting data) and **hashing** (for securing passwords). Encryption ensures that even if someone gains access to your data, they can't read it, while hashing ensures that sensitive data (like passwords) is stored securely.

Best Practices: Writing Secure, Efficient Java Code

Writing secure Java code is crucial to preventing vulnerabilities that could be exploited by attackers. Here are some essential best practices for writing secure and efficient Java applications:

1. Validate User Input

Never trust user input. Always validate and sanitize input to prevent attacks like SQL injection and XSS. Use built-in libraries to handle input validation and escaping.

- **SQL Injection Protection**: Use **PreparedStatements** instead of **Statement** objects to avoid directly concatenating user input into SQL queries.

```java
```

```
String sql = "SELECT * FROM users WHERE username
= ?";
PreparedStatement              ps              =
connection.prepareStatement(sql);
ps.setString(1, username);
ResultSet rs = ps.executeQuery();
```

- **HTML Escaping**: When displaying user-generated content in HTML, always escape special characters to prevent XSS attacks.

2. Use Strong Passwords and Hashing

Never store passwords as plain text. Always use a strong hashing algorithm, such as **bcrypt** or **PBKDF2**, to hash passwords before storing them. Use **salt** to add additional randomness to the hashed passwords.

3. Implement Secure Session Management

Use **secure, HttpOnly**, and **SameSite** flags on cookies to ensure session identifiers are protected. Avoid using predictable session identifiers, and regenerate session IDs after login to prevent session fixation attacks.

4. Use Secure Communication (SSL/TLS)

Always encrypt sensitive data transmitted over the network by using **SSL/TLS**. This ensures that data such as passwords and personal information is securely transmitted between the client and server.

```java
System.setProperty("https.protocols",
"TLSv1.2");
```

5. Avoid Hardcoding Secrets

Do not hardcode sensitive information such as passwords or API keys directly in your code. Use secure ways to store secrets, such as environment variables or external configuration files, and ensure these files are properly protected.

6. Limit Access and Use Principle of Least Privilege

Limit access to sensitive operations and data using role-based access control (RBAC). Follow the **Principle of Least Privilege**, granting only the minimum level of access required for each user or component.

Practical Example: Implementing Password Hashing and Encryption in a Java Application

Now let's implement **password hashing and encryption** in a Java application using the **Java Cryptography Architecture**

(**JCA**). In this example, we will hash a password using **SHA-256** (a secure hashing algorithm) and encrypt/decrypt data using **AES** (Advanced Encryption Standard).

Step 1: Password Hashing with SHA-256

To securely store passwords, you should hash them before storing them in the database. The MessageDigest class from Java's standard library can be used for hashing.

```java
import java.security.MessageDigest;
import java.security.NoSuchAlgorithmException;

public class PasswordUtils {

    public static String hashPassword(String password) {
        try {
            // Create a MessageDigest instance for SHA-256
            MessageDigest digest = MessageDigest.getInstance("SHA-256");

            // Hash the password
            byte[] hashedBytes = digest.digest(password.getBytes());
```

```
            // Convert the byte array into a
hexadecimal string
            StringBuilder hexString = new
StringBuilder();
            for (byte b : hashedBytes) {

hexString.append(String.format("%02x", b));
            }

            return hexString.toString();    //
Return the hashed password
        } catch (NoSuchAlgorithmException e) {
            e.printStackTrace();
        }
        return null;
    }

    public static void main(String[] args) {
        String password =
"mySecurePassword123!";
        String hashedPassword =
hashPassword(password);
        System.out.println("Hashed Password: " +
hashedPassword);
    }
}
```

- **MessageDigest.getInstance("SHA-256")**:
  Creates a `MessageDigest` object for hashing using the SHA-256 algorithm.
- The password is hashed using `digest()` and returned as a hexadecimal string.

Step 2: Password Encryption and Decryption with AES

For encrypting sensitive data, such as personal information or messages, you can use **AES encryption**. The following example demonstrates how to encrypt and decrypt data with AES.

java

```java
import javax.crypto.Cipher;
import javax.crypto.KeyGenerator;
import javax.crypto.SecretKey;
import javax.crypto.spec.SecretKeySpec;
import java.util.Base64;

public class EncryptionUtils {

    // Encrypt data using AES
    public static String encrypt(String data,
String key) throws Exception {
        SecretKeySpec    secretKey    =    new
SecretKeySpec(key.getBytes(), "AES");
        Cipher            cipher           =
Cipher.getInstance("AES");
```

```java
        cipher.init(Cipher.ENCRYPT_MODE,
secretKey);
        byte[]              encryptedData       =
cipher.doFinal(data.getBytes());
        return
Base64.getEncoder().encodeToString(encryptedDat
a); // Encode to base64 for easy display
    }


    // Decrypt data using AES
    public    static    String    decrypt(String
encryptedData, String key) throws Exception {
        SecretKeySpec    secretKey    =    new
SecretKeySpec(key.getBytes(), "AES");
        Cipher            cipher            =
Cipher.getInstance("AES");
        cipher.init(Cipher.DECRYPT_MODE,
secretKey);
        byte[]              decodedData         =
Base64.getDecoder().decode(encryptedData);
        byte[]              decryptedData       =
cipher.doFinal(decodedData);
        return new String(decryptedData);
    }


    public static void main(String[] args) {
        try {
            String key = "1234567890123456"; //
16-byte AES key (128-bit)
```

```
        String    originalData  -  "Sensitive
Information";

        // Encrypt the data
        String        encryptedData        =
encrypt(originalData, key);
        System.out.println("Encrypted Data:
" + encryptedData);

        // Decrypt the data
        String        decryptedData        =
decrypt(encryptedData, key);
        System.out.println("Decrypted Data:
" + decryptedData);
      } catch (Exception e) {
        e.printStackTrace();
      }
    }
}
```

- **AES Encryption**: We use a 16-byte key (128-bit) to encrypt and decrypt the data. The data is first converted into a byte array, encrypted, and then encoded in **Base64** for easier representation.
- **Decryption**: The encrypted data is decoded and then decrypted using the same key.

Conclusion

In this chapter, we explored **Java Security** and **best practices** for building secure Java applications. We learned about common security threats like SQL injection, XSS, and CSRF, and how Java provides tools like **JCA** for encryption and hashing to secure sensitive data.

We implemented **password hashing** using SHA-256 and **data encryption** using AES, demonstrating how you can protect user credentials and sensitive information in your applications.

By following the best practices outlined in this chapter, such as input validation, secure session management, and encryption, you can write secure, efficient Java applications that protect your data and users.

In the next chapters, we will explore more advanced topics in Java security, including **authentication mechanisms**, **secure coding techniques**, and how to integrate **Spring Security** for more comprehensive application security.

CHAPTER 26

WORKING WITH EXTERNAL LIBRARIES AND APIS

What are APIs? How to Interact with External APIs Using Java

An **API (Application Programming Interface)** is a set of rules and protocols that allow different software applications to communicate with each other. APIs define the methods and data formats that applications can use to request services or share data. APIs allow developers to access features or data from external services, such as weather data, payment gateways, social media, and more, without needing to know the internal workings of those services.

APIs can be:

- **RESTful APIs**: These are based on HTTP and use standard HTTP methods like GET, POST, PUT, and DELETE to perform operations. They typically return data in JSON or XML format.
- **SOAP APIs**: These use XML for communication and are typically used in enterprise applications.

- **WebSocket APIs**: These are used for real-time, two-way communication between a client and server.

In Java, you can interact with **RESTful APIs** using standard libraries like **HttpURLConnection**, **HttpClient**, or third-party libraries like **Apache HttpClient** or **OkHttp**.

Using External Libraries: Integrating Third-Party Libraries into Your Java Projects

External libraries are pre-built collections of classes and functions that provide reusable code for specific functionality. These libraries are often open-source or commercially available and can save you time and effort by handling common tasks such as HTTP requests, JSON parsing, or database interaction.

1. Adding Libraries to Your Project

There are several ways to add external libraries to your Java project, depending on the build tool you're using.

- **Maven**: Maven is a build automation tool used to manage project dependencies. You can add external libraries by specifying them in your `pom.xml` file.

Example: To use **Apache HttpClient** in Maven, add the following dependency:

```xml
xml

<dependency>

<groupId>org.apache.httpcomponents</groupId>
    <artifactId>httpclient</artifactId>
    <version>4.5.13</version>
</dependency>
```

- **Gradle**: Gradle is another build tool used for managing dependencies. You can add libraries by including them in your `build.gradle` file.

  Example: To use **OkHttp** in Gradle, add the following dependency:

```gradle
gradle

implementation
'com.squareup.okhttp3:okhttp:4.9.0'
```

- **Manual JARs**: If you're not using a build tool, you can manually download the JAR files of the libraries and add them to your project's classpath.

2. Popular External Libraries in Java

- **Jackson/Gson**: Libraries for parsing and converting JSON data.
- **Apache HttpClient**: A popular library for making HTTP requests.
- **OkHttp**: Another popular HTTP client that is efficient and easy to use.
- **SLF4J**: A logging facade that allows you to use different logging frameworks.
- **JUnit**: A widely-used framework for unit testing Java applications.

Practical Example: Fetching and Displaying Weather Data from a Public API

In this example, we will use a public API to fetch weather data. We'll interact with the **OpenWeatherMap API**, which provides weather information for different cities around the world. To keep things simple, we'll use **HttpURLConnection**, a built-in Java class, to make HTTP requests.

Step 1: Sign Up for OpenWeatherMap API

1. Go to OpenWeatherMap and create a free account.

2. After signing up, you'll get an **API Key** which you'll need to authenticate your requests.

Step 2: Set Up Your Java Project

If you are using Maven, add the following dependencies in your pom.xml to handle JSON parsing:

xml

```
<dependency>

<groupId>com.fasterxml.jackson.core</groupId>
    <artifactId>jackson-databind</artifactId>
    <version>2.12.3</version>
</dependency>
```

If you're using Gradle, add this line to your build.gradle file:

gradle

```
implementation
'com.fasterxml.jackson.core:jackson-
databind:2.12.3'
```

Step 3: Write Java Code to Fetch Weather Data

Now we will write the Java code to fetch weather data for a specific city.

Java Code:

java

```java
import java.io.BufferedReader;
import java.io.InputStreamReader;
import java.net.HttpURLConnection;
import java.net.URL;
import com.fasterxml.jackson.databind.JsonNode;
import com.fasterxml.jackson.databind.ObjectMapper;

public class WeatherFetcher {

    private static final String API_KEY = "YOUR_API_KEY";    // Replace with your OpenWeatherMap API key
    private static final String BASE_URL = "http://api.openweathermap.org/data/2.5/weather?q=";

    // Method to fetch weather data for a city
    public static String getWeather(String city) {
        try {
            // Build the URL for the API request
            String urlString = BASE_URL + city + "&appid=" + API_KEY + "&units=metric";    // units=metric for Celsius
            URL url = new URL(urlString);
```

```java
        // Create an HttpURLConnection
object to connect to the API
        HttpURLConnection connection =
(HttpURLConnection) url.openConnection();
        connection.setRequestMethod("GET");

        // Read the response from the API
        BufferedReader in = new
BufferedReader(new
InputStreamReader(connection.getInputStream()))
;
        String inputLine;
        StringBuilder response = new
StringBuilder();
        while ((inputLine = in.readLine())
!= null) {
            response.append(inputLine);
        }
        in.close();

        // Parse the JSON response
        ObjectMapper objectMapper = new
ObjectMapper();
        JsonNode rootNode =
objectMapper.readTree(response.toString());
        JsonNode mainNode =
rootNode.path("main");
```

```java
                double         temperature         =
mainNode.path("temp").asDouble();
                double         humidity         =
mainNode.path("humidity").asDouble();

                // Return the formatted weather
information
                return   String.format("Temperature:
%.2f°C\nHumidity:    %.2f%%",         temperature,
humidity);

        } catch (Exception e) {
            e.printStackTrace();
            return   "Error   fetching   weather
data.";
        }
    }

    public static void main(String[] args) {
        // Example city: "London"
        String city = "London";
        String weatherData = getWeather(city);
        System.out.println("Weather data for " +
city + ":\n" + weatherData);
    }
}
```

Explanation of the Code:

1. **API URL**: The URL to the OpenWeatherMap API is constructed with the city name and your API key.

2. **HTTP Request**: We use `HttpURLConnection` to send a GET request to the OpenWeatherMap API.

3. **Response Handling**: The response is read line by line using `BufferedReader` and stored in a `StringBuilder`.

4. **JSON Parsing**: We use Jackson's `ObjectMapper` to parse the JSON response into a `JsonNode`. The weather data (temperature and humidity) is extracted from the response.

5. **Output**: The temperature and humidity are formatted and printed to the console.

Step 4: Run the Application

When you run the application, it will fetch the current weather data for the specified city and display it in the console.

Example Output:

```yaml
Weather data for London:
Temperature: 15.23°C
Humidity: 82.00%
```

313

Conclusion

In this chapter, we explored how to interact with **external APIs** in Java. We used the **OpenWeatherMap API** to fetch weather data, demonstrating how to send HTTP requests, handle JSON responses, and display the data in a user-friendly format.

We also discussed the process of **integrating external libraries** like **Jackson** to simplify tasks like JSON parsing. This example highlights how powerful APIs are for enhancing Java applications by providing access to external data and services.

In the next chapters, we will explore more advanced topics related to integrating Java with external systems, such as working with **RESTful APIs**, **authentication** with OAuth, and **integrating Java with third-party libraries** for various use cases.

CHAPTER 27

FINAL PROJECT: BUILDING A COMPLETE JAVA APPLICATION

Putting It All Together: A Capstone Project That Integrates Everything You've Learned

In this chapter, you will apply everything you've learned throughout the course by building a **complete Java application**. This final project serves as a capstone, allowing you to put together concepts like **object-oriented programming (OOP)**, **database integration (JDBC)**, **web development (JavaFX, Spring Boot)**, **security**, **API interaction**, and **performance optimization** into a fully functional application.

For this project, we will focus on building a **full-fledged e-commerce platform**. This platform will allow users to browse products, add them to a cart, proceed to checkout, and manage orders. We will use technologies like **Spring Boot**, **JavaFX**, **JDBC**, **RESTful APIs**, **security practices**, and more to make the application robust and scalable.

Designing the Application: Planning, Coding, and Testing the Final Java Project

1. Planning the Application

Before you start coding, it is crucial to **plan** the application's structure, features, and design. This involves:

- **Defining the features**: List the functionalities that your e-commerce platform should have, such as user authentication, product catalog, cart management, checkout, and order tracking.
- **Choosing the right technologies**: Decide whether to build a web-based application (using **Spring Boot** for the backend and **JavaFX** for the front-end) or a mobile app (using **JavaFX** with a mobile-compatible framework).
- **Database Design**: Identify the tables needed for your database (e.g., users, products, orders, payments) and their relationships.
- **UI Design**: Plan the user interface, either using **JavaFX** for desktop or HTML/CSS for web-based applications.

2. Architecture and Components

For a typical e-commerce platform, the architecture might consist of:

- **Frontend**: The user interface where customers browse products and manage their cart.
  - **JavaFX** or **React** (for a web application).
- **Backend**: The business logic, including handling orders, payments, and customer management.
  - **Spring Boot** or **Java EE**.
- **Database**: Where product, user, and order data is stored.
  - **MySQL**, **PostgreSQL**, or **SQLite**.
- **Security**: Implementing user authentication and authorization.
  - **JWT tokens**, **Spring Security**, **password hashing**.
- **APIs**: Allowing interaction with external systems (e.g., payment gateways, weather services).
  - **RESTful APIs** for payment processing, shipping, and product updates.

Practical Example: Building a Full-Fledged E-Commerce Website with Java

Let's build the basic backend structure for an e-commerce application using **Spring Boot** for the backend, **JDBC** for database integration, and **Spring Security** for handling authentication.

317

Step 1: Setting Up the Project

You can set up the project using **Spring Initializr** (https://start.spring.io/) or manually by creating a Maven or Gradle-based project with dependencies for **Spring Boot**, **JDBC**, **Spring Security**, and **Thymeleaf** (for the view layer if using Spring MVC).

Dependencies:

- **Spring Web** (for building the REST API).
- **Spring Data JPA** or **JDBC** (for database access).
- **Spring Security** (for authentication).
- **Thymeleaf** (if using Spring MVC for frontend).
- **H2** or **MySQL** (for the database).

Step 2: Create the Product and User Models

Let's define the **Product** and **User** entities.

Product.java:

```java

package com.example.ecommerce.model;

import javax.persistence.Entity;
import javax.persistence.GeneratedValue;
```

318

```java
import javax.persistence.Id;

@Entity
public class Product {
    @Id
    @GeneratedValue
    private Long id;
    private String name;
    private double price;
    private String description;

    // Constructor, getters, and setters
    public Product() {}

    public Product(String name, double price,
String description) {
        this.name = name;
        this.price = price;
        this.description = description;
    }

    public Long getId() {
        return id;
    }

    public void setId(Long id) {
        this.id = id;
    }
```

```java
    public String getName() {
        return name;
    }

    public void setName(String name) {
        this.name = name;
    }

    public double getPrice() {
        return price;
    }

    public void setPrice(double price) {
        this.price = price;
    }

    public String getDescription() {
        return description;
    }

    public      void      setDescription(String
description) {
        this.description = description;
    }
}
```

User.java:

```
java
```

```java
package com.example.ecommerce.model;

import javax.persistence.Entity;
import javax.persistence.GeneratedValue;
import javax.persistence.Id;

@Entity
public class User {
    @Id
    @GeneratedValue
    private Long id;
    private String username;
    private String password;

    // Constructor, getters, and setters
    public User() {}

    public   User(String   username,   String
password) {
        this.username = username;
        this.password = password;
    }

    public Long getId() {
        return id;
    }

    public void setId(Long id) {
        this.id = id;
```

```java
    }

    public String getUsername() {
        return username;
    }

    public void setUsername(String username) {
        this.username = username;
    }

    public String getPassword() {
        return password;
    }

    public void setPassword(String password) {
        this.password = password;
    }
}
```

Step 3: Database Integration with JDBC

Create the **ProductRepository** and **UserRepository** to handle CRUD operations using **JDBC**.

ProductRepository.java:

```java
java
```

```java
package com.example.ecommerce.repository;
```

```java
import com.example.ecommerce.model.Product;
import
org.springframework.stereotype.Repository;
import javax.sql.DataSource;
import java.sql.*;
import java.util.ArrayList;
import java.util.List;

@Repository
public class ProductRepository {

    private final DataSource dataSource;

    public          ProductRepository(DataSource
dataSource) {
        this.dataSource = dataSource;
    }

    public List<Product> getAllProducts() {
        List<Product>    products    =    new
ArrayList<>();
        String query = "SELECT * FROM products";
        try    (Connection    connection    =
dataSource.getConnection();
            PreparedStatement    statement    =
connection.prepareStatement(query);
            ResultSet          resultSet          =
statement.executeQuery()) {
```

```java
        while (resultSet.next()) {
            Product product = new Product(

resultSet.getString("name"),

resultSet.getDouble("price"),

resultSet.getString("description")
                );
                products.add(product);
            }
        } catch (SQLException e) {
            e.printStackTrace();
        }
        return products;
    }


    // Other CRUD methods (e.g., save, update,
delete) can be added here
}
```

UserRepository.java:

java

```java
package com.example.ecommerce.repository;

import com.example.ecommerce.model.User;
import
org.springframework.stereotype.Repository;
```

```java
import javax.sql.DataSource;
import java.sql.*;

@Repository
public class UserRepository {

    private final DataSource dataSource;

    public UserRepository(DataSource dataSource)
{
        this.dataSource = dataSource;
    }

    public     User     getUserByUsername(String
username) {
        String query = "SELECT * FROM users WHERE
username = ?";
        try     (Connection     connection     =
dataSource.getConnection();
            PreparedStatement     statement     =
connection.prepareStatement(query)) {
            statement.setString(1, username);
            try     (ResultSet     resultSet     =
statement.executeQuery()) {
                if (resultSet.next()) {
                    return new User(

resultSet.getString("username"),
```

```
resultSet.getString("password")
                );
            }
        }
    } catch (SQLException e) {
        e.printStackTrace();
    }
    return null;
    }
}
```

Step 4: Security with Spring Security

Configure **Spring Security** to manage user authentication. You can add basic authentication or token-based authentication using JWT (JSON Web Tokens).

Security Configuration (Example: Basic Authentication):

WebSecurityConfig.java:

```
java
```

```
package com.example.ecommerce.config;

import
org.springframework.context.annotation.Configur
ation;
```

```
import
org.springframework.security.config.annotation.
web.builders.HttpSecurity;
import
org.springframework.security.config.annotation.
web.configuration.EnableWebSecurity;
import
org.springframework.security.config.annotation.
web.configuration.WebSecurityConfigurerAdapter;

@Configuration
@EnableWebSecurity
public    class    WebSecurityConfig    extends
WebSecurityConfigurerAdapter {

    @Override
    protected void configure(HttpSecurity http)
throws Exception {
        http
            .authorizeRequests()
            .antMatchers("/login",
"/register").permitAll()
            .anyRequest().authenticated()
            .and()
            .formLogin()
            .loginPage("/login")
            .permitAll()
            .and()
            .logout()
```

```
        .permitAll();
    }
}
```

Step 5: Implementing the Cart and Checkout System

Create an application that allows users to add products to their cart, view the cart, and proceed to checkout.

- **Cart**: The cart will store the products the user adds.
- **Checkout**: The checkout system will calculate the total price and simulate the payment process.

Conclusion

In this chapter, you learned how to build a **complete Java application** by applying concepts like **Spring Boot, JDBC, Spring Security**, and **database management** to create a full-fledged **e-commerce platform**. You gained experience with setting up models, creating repositories, handling authentication, and securing your application.

As you continue building this project, you can extend it by adding more advanced features such as **payment integration, order tracking**, and **real-time notifications**.

In the next chapters, we will explore further aspects of Java development, including advanced **RESTful APIs, microservices architectures**, and **scalable web applications**.

www.ingramcontent.com/pod-product-compliance
Lightning Source LLC
LaVergne TN
LVHW051431050326
832903LV00030BD/3017